CBSE Board Exams 2023

Information Technology

Class 10

CBSE Board Exams 2023

10 Sample Question Papers

As Per Latest CBSE Sample Paper Issued on 16 Sep. 2022

Information Technology

Class 10

Author
Suhasini Tiwari
B.Tech. (Information Technology)

Arihant Prakashan (School Division Series)

*arihant

Arihant Prakashan (School Division Series)

ॐ **Administrative & Production Offices**

Regd. Office
'Ramchhaya' 4577/15, Agarwal Road, Darya Ganj, New Delhi -110002
Tele: 011- 47630600, 43518550

ॐ **Head Office**
Kalindi, TP Nagar, Meerut (UP) - 250002
Tel: 0121-7156203, 7156204

ॐ **Sales & Support Offices**
Agra, Ahmedabad, Bengaluru, Bareilly, Chennai, Delhi, Guwahati, Hyderabad, Jaipur, Jhansi, Kolkata, Lucknow, Nagpur & Pune.

ॐ **PRICE** ₹115.00

PO No : TXT-XX-XXXXXXX-X-XX

Published by Arihant Publications (India) Ltd.

For further information about the books published by Arihant, log on to www.arihantbooks.com or e-mail at info@arihantbooks.com

Follow us on   

REAL PRACTICE
A Key to Achieve Perfection

Practice is the key to achieve perfection; one should practice to achieve perfection in any field and school examinations are not an exception to this fact. Constant practice can help one to overcome his weakness. The practice done in a right way with proper guidelines helps to attain grasp over the subject and result in a 'Perfect Performance'.

Sample paper is a must have study resource for each and every student, as it helps them to make themselves acquainted with the real exam paper pattern. They can check and update different aspects like enough speed to complete the paper within the prescribed time limit, identifying those topics/chapter, they are not comfortable with, polishing their skills of writing the answer as per the need of the question, etc.

i Succeed 10 Sample Question Papers will serve the above cited purpose in a perfect manner. This book will help you to master all the skills required to attempt the CBSE Class X Examination Paper perfectly. This series is not just another Sample Paper series in the market, there are some special features associated with *i Succeed* which make it stand apart.

Some of them are :

o A special section at the start, **The Qualifying Round** to give you an assessment of your Chapterwise Knowledge before attempting the full length Sample Question Papers.

o For Step-by-Step Upgradation, Sample Question Papers grouped into **Three Stages: Stage I, II & III**. Through these stages one can enhance his/her performance gradually .

o All Sample Papers are according to pattern of **Latest CBSE Sample Paper.**

o At the end, there are fully solved **Latest CBSE Sample Paper** & a separate sample paper for **One Day Before Exam.**

To gain maximum benefit from Sample Papers, it is advised that you attempt the papers at a stretch in 2 hours without any help.

Although, I have put my best efforts to preparing this book, but if any error or discrepancy has skipped my attention, or you have any suggestion, send your feedbacks. I will welcome your feedback. I thank everyone involved in the process of preparing this book and especially acknowledge the contribution of Shruti Aggarwal (Project Coordinator). With the hope that this book will be of great help to the students, I wish great success to my readers.

Author
Suhasini Tiwari

STAGES
of Real Practice

COURSE STRUCTURE
2022-23 (Code 402)

The unit-wise distribution of hours and marks for Class X is as follow

	Units	No. of Hours for Theory and Practical 200		Max. Marks for Theory and Practical 100
	Employability Skills			
	Unit 1: Communication Skills-II*	10		-
	Unit 2: Self-Management Skills-II	10		3
PART A	Unit 3: ICT Skills-II	10		3
	Unit 4: Entrepreneurial Skills-II	15		4
	Unit 5: Green Skills-II*	05		-
	Total	50		**10**
	Subject Specific Skills	**Theory (In Hours)**	**Practical (In Hours)**	**Marks**
	Unit 1: Digital Documentation (Advanced)	12	18	8
	Unit 2: Electronic Spreadsheet (Advanced)	15	23	10
PART B	Unit 3: Database Management System	18	27	12
	Unit 4: Web Applications and Security	15	22	10
	Total	**60**	**90**	**40**
	Practical Work			**Marks**
	Practical Examination			
PART C	• Advanced Documentation	5 Marks		
	• Advanced Spreadsheets	5 Marks		20
	• Databases	10 Marks		
	• Viva Voce	10 Marks		10
	Total			**30**

	Project Work/Field Visit		Marks
PART D	Any Interdisciplinary Real World Case Study to be taken. Summarized data reports of same can be presented in base. Input should be taken using forms and output should be done using reports using base. Documentation of the case study should be presented using writer.		10
	PORTFOLIO/ PRACTICAL FILE: (Portfolio should contain printouts of the practical done using Writer, Calc and Base with minimum 5 problems of each)		10
	Total		**20**
	Grand Total	**200**	**100**

**Note: * marked units are to be assessed through Internal Assessment/ Student Activities.
They are not to be assessed in Theory Exams**

BLUE-PRINT

For Sample Question Paper for Class X

Max. Time : 2 Hours
Max. Marks : 50

PART A - EMPLOYABILITY SKILLS (10 MARKS)

UNIT NO.	NAME OF THE UNIT	OBJECTIVE TYPE QUESTIONS	SHORT ANSWER TYPE QUESTIONS	TOTAL QUESTIONS
		1 MARK EACH	2 MARKS EACH	
1	Communication Skills - II	-	-	-
2	Self- Management Skills - II	2	2	4
3	ICT Skills - II	2	1	3
4	Entrepreneurial Skills - II	2	2	4
5	Green Skills - II	-	-	-
	TOTAL QUESTIONS	6	5	11
	NO. OF QUESTIONS TO BE ANSWERED	Any 4	Any 3	07
	TOTAL MARKS	1 x 4 = 4	2 x 3 = 6	10 MARKS

PART B - SUBJECT SPECIFIC SKILLS (40 MARKS)

UNIT NO.	NAME OF THE UNIT	OBJECTIVE TYPE QUESTIONS	SHORT ANSWER TYPE QUESTIONS	DESCRIPTIVE/ LONG ANS. TYPE QUESTIONS	TOTAL QUESTIONS
		1 MARK EACH	2 MARKS EACH	4 MARKS EACH	
	Digital Documentation (Advanced)	6	1	1	8
	Electronic Spreadsheet (Advanced)	6	2	1	9
	Database Management System	6	1	2	9
	Web Applications and Security	6	2	1	9
	TOTAL QUESTIONS	24	6	5	35
	NO. OF QUESTIONS TO BE ANSWERED	20	Any 4	Any 3	27
	TOTAL MARKS	1 x 20 = 20	2 x 4 = 8	4 x 3 = 12	40 MARKS

Qualifying ROUND

<u>Part A</u> **Employability Skills**

Unit-1 : Communication Skills-II

1. Verbal communication consists of .... communication and .... communication.

2. A word used to express emotions and is often followed by an exclamation mark is called ....

3. What does a predicate in a sentence refer to?

4. Describe what we mean by encoding a message.

5. Describe the following terms:
   (i) Transmission of message
   (ii) Feedback

6. What are semantics barriers?

7. Differentiate between specific and non-specific feedback with examples.

8. What measures can be ensured so that barriers to communication do not arise?

9. There are 7C's of effective communication. List all of them.

10. Explain the parts of a sentence with examples.

Unit-2 : Self-Management Skills-II

1. .... focuses on your ability to influence personal and professional improvement based on your self-awareness and motivation.

2. ...., is a result of pent-up worries.

3. How leisure activities benefit in stress management?

4. What are some of the factors that cause stress?

5. Describe fight-or-flight response.

6. How does meditation help in overcoming stress?

7. What is the alarm response? Explain

8. Independent working requires skills. Mention a few of them.

9. There are different types of stress. Write about them.

10. Describe why self-awareness is important and how does it help us. Also, mention the kinds of self-awareness.

Unit-3 : Basic ICT Skills-II

1. ...... is a word processing feature that forces all text to be confined within defined margins.

2. .... is a software application capable of organising, storing and analysing data in tabular form.

3. How can you save and print a presentation?

4. Describe the following features of Calc:
   (i) Resizing fonts and styles
   (ii) Formulas and functions

5. John protected his file through a password. Now, he wants to remove it. Help him by describing the correct sequence of the steps to remove password.

6. Why do we need a word processor? Name a few softwares useful for word processing.

7. How does the Find and Replace feature help us? Explain.

8. Describe the role of Slide Transition and Slide Animation in creating an impressive presentation.

9. What are the features offered by a presentation software? Describe in detail.

10. How can a new worksheet be created in calc? Mention any four features of Open Office Calc.

Unit-4 : Entrepreneurial Skills-II

1. The entrepreneur creates maximum .... opportunities in the society.

2. .... and .... are the qualities of a good leader.

3. Who is an enterpreneur? Define the term entrepreneurship.

4. Write about any two functions of an entrepreneur.

5. Write about any four qualities of an entrepreneur in order to run a successful enterprise.

6. Describe why are entrepreneurs significant?

7. Mention a few advantages of enterpreneurship as a career.

8. Describe how uncertain income and incompetent staff are disadvantageous to entrepreneurship.

9. Ravi has established an enterprise. Describe how he would generate employment opportunities and develop new production techniques.

10. Write about the most common myths of entrepreneurship.

Unit-5 : Green Skills-II

1. .... and .... can protect ecology.

2. The most significant environmental problems are associated with resources that are ....

3. How has Brundtland Report defined sustainable development?

4. Write about any two challenges to sustainable development.

5. What are the requirements to achieve sustainable developlent?

6. Why is sustainable development necessary? Explain.

7. What are a few short term solutions related to sustainable development?

8. Describe the goals set by United Nations sustainable Development Summit (2015) for sustainable development.

9. Explain the problems and solutions related to sustainable development.

10. Describe in detail the importance of sustainable development.

Part B   Subject Skills

Unit-1 : Digital Documentation (Advanced)

1. .... alignment is used to align all the selected text equal from both the sides.

2. You can make your documents professional and polished by utilising the ...... and ...... sections.

3. How to insert a text into a template?

4. Differentiate between odd page break and even page break.

5. Jai has created a header area in his document. List any five items that he can add to it.

6. Sushila is using a word processor object. What options does word processor object?

7. There are different types of text case options. Describe them.

8. Write some features of spelling checker in open office writer.

9. Elucidate the significance of modifying the spacing of the lines or paragraph of text.

10. Ram wants to compress a picture. Write the steps through which he can do so.

Unit-2 : Electronic Spreadsheet (Advanced)

1. ......, ... and ...... are three types of cell referencing.

2. ...... are tool test for what if questions.

3. How are workbook views useful in Excel?

4. Define relative referencing. Write the formula for adding values of cells A1 to A5.

5. How do you freeze rows and columns in a spreadsheet?

6. Mention the purpose of pie charts in Excel.

7. How many types of chart elements are available in an electronic spreadsheet? Explain.

8. Write the steps for identifying dupilcates in excel?

9. Explain the concept of workbook views along with its various types.

10. The workbooks can be linked with the help of External data or the navigator.

Unit-3 : Database Management System

1. ...... is an alternate key which is not used as primary key.

2. ...... provides characters upto 65536 so, it is used for long text entries.

3. How is DDL different from DML?

4. How many types of users are there in a schema?

5. Raghuveer wishes to create a table in his database. What rules should he keep in mind to do so?

6. How is a foreign key different from primary key? Explain.

7. Define the following :
   (i) Auto number   (ii) Currency   (iii) Text

8. Explain the significance of using queries in database.

9. Differentiate a record from a field with examples.

10. How does DBMS prove to be useful in a hospital? What is DML? Explain.

Unit-4 : Web Applications and Security

1. .... is a small area network created around a bluetooth device.

2. ...... type of software is accessed using browsers.

3. The address of location of the document on WWW is called ......

4. Define networking. What are the main types of computer networks?

5. Describe the following devices:
   (i) Router   (ii)   Modem

6. Why is networking beneficial to us? Explain.

7. How is circuit switching different from packet switching? Why is a repeater used in a network?

8. What is browser? Also, explain the types of browsers.

9. What is blog? Also, write the steps to create a Blog account in WordPress.

10. Explain the various high speed transmission technologies that broadband offers.

SAMPLE QUESTION PAPER 1

Information Technology

Time : **2 hrs**   Max. Marks : **50**

Instructions

1. Please read the instructions carefully
2. This Question Paper consists of 21 questions in two sections: Section A & Section B.
3. Section A has Objective type questions whereas Section B contains Subjective type questions.
4. Out of the given (5 + 16 =) 21 questions, a candidate has to answer (5 + 10 =) 15 questions in the allotted (maximum) time of 2 hours.
5. All questions of a particular section must be attempted in the correct order.
6. Section A : Objective Type Questions (24 Marks)
    (i) This section has 05 questions.
    (ii) Marks allotted are mentioned against each question/part.
    (iii) There is no negative marking.
    (iv) Do as per the instructions given.
7. Section B: Subjective Type Questions (26 Marks)
    (i) This section has 16 questions.
    (ii) A candidate has to do 10 questions.
    (iii) Do as per the instructions given.
    (iv) Marks allotted are mentioned against each question/part.

Section-A

(Objective Type Questions)

1. Answer any 4 out of the given 6 questions based on Employability Skills   [1 × 4 = 4 Marks]

(i) Identify the measure to protect computer from tand viruses.   [1]

    (a) Sharing password with friends   (b) Allow anyone to use your device

    (c) Use Antivirus   (d) Leave computer without logging out

Ans. (c) Use Antivirus

(ii) .... means communication through spoken and written words.   [1]
    (a) Non-verbal communication   (b) Feedback
    (c) Verbal communication   (d) None of these

Ans. (c) Verbal communication

(iii) .... is our body's way of responding to any kind of demand.   [1]
    (a) Stress   (b) Self-regulation
    (c) Self-motivation   (d) All of these

Ans. (a) Stress

(iv) A/ An .... has to create a spirit of team work and motivate them.   [1]
    (a) entrepreneur   (b) government policy
    (c) Both (a) and (b)   (d) None of these

Ans. (a) entrepreneur

(v) A .... operating system is a computing environment that reacts to input within a specific
period of time.   [1]
    (a) single-user   (b) real time   (c) multi-user   (d) distribute

Ans. (b) real time

(vi) Which of the following is necessary for the maintenance of the environment?   [1]
    (a) Poor management   (b) Sustainable development
    (c) Man made resources   (d) None of these

Ans. (b) Sustainable development

2. Answer any 5 out of the given 6 questions   [1 × 5 = 5 Marks]

(i) Which of the following is an application program that is stored on a remote server and delivered
over the Internet?   [1]
    (a) Web application   (b) System application
    (c) Internet application   (d) None of the above

Ans. (a) Web application

(ii) Which of the following is not a good choice as a field name for a database?   [1]
    (a) Emp_Id   (b) Emp_dept
    (c) Emp_name   (d) Emp_set

Ans. (d) Emp _set

(iii) The data in the data source is organised in   [1]
    (a) text form   (b) image form
    (c) tabular form   (d) paragraph form

Ans. (c) tabular form

(iv) Shalini is working in a school. She is the class teacher of VIII B. It is the time to enter the subject
marks and grades of all students of her class in a worksheet. While entering the marks and
grades, she has to scroll up again and again to the row where all subject names are entered, in
order to avoid any mistakes in her entries. This process is consuming a lot of her time. Help her by
letting her know about one such tool by which she can fix the field rows from the following and
continue with her work without wasting much time.   [1]
    (a) Fix row   (b) Fix column
    (c) Freeze panes   (d) Freeze all

Ans. (c) Freeze panes

(v) Template is a .... document based on which one can create a new document.   [1]
    (a) blueprint   (b) printed   (c) suggested   (d) copied

Ans. (a) blueprint

(vi) Which of the following is not an object of a database? [1]

   (a)Report   (b) Forms   (c) Query   (d) Functions

Ans. (d) Functions

3. Answer any 5 out of the given 6 questions   [1 × 5 = 5 Marks]

   (i) Grouping drawing object can be used for which of the following? [1]

     (a) Combining drawing objects as one   (b) Resizing

     (c) Adding more drawing objects   (d) None of these

Ans. (a) Combining drawing objects as one

   (ii) Aanya is making a table in Access to store data of all the employees working in her organisation. She has decided on the various information that she needs to store in that table. She also has to have a field in which only unique data can be entered. Out of the given fields suggest the best field suitable that can be used as a primary key, so that it can accept only unique data. [1]

     (a) Emp_name   (b) Emp_dept   (c) Emp_number   (d) Emp_DOB

Ans. (c) Emp_number

   (iii) Computer connected with LAN [1]

     (a) can work fast   (b) can go online

     (c) can E-mail   (d) can share information or peripheral devices

Ans. (d) can share information or peripheral devices

   (iv) State True or False.

     "A custom style displays user-defined styles." [1]

     (a) True   (b) False

Ans. (a) True

   (v) According to Open Office Calc which of the following is not a What-if analysis tool? [1]

     (a) Conditional formatting   (b) Goal seek

     (c) Scenarios   (d) Solver

Ans. (b) Goal Seek

   (vi) .... allows multiple users to view, edit and change in a spreadsheet. [1]

     (a) Opening   (b) Reviewing

     (c) Sharing   (d) Collaborating

Ans. (c) Sharing

4. Answer any 5 out of the given 6 questions   [1 × 5 = 5 Marks]

   (i) What can you do with the Internet? [1]

     (a) Exchange information with friends and colleagues.

     (b) Access pictures, sounds, video clips and other media elements.

     (c) Find diverse perspective on issues from a global audience.

     (d) All of the above

Ans. (d) All of the above

   (ii) The Show Changes dialog box has which of the following settings? [1]

     (a) Data   (b) Comment   (c) Views   (d) All of these

Ans. (d) All of these

   (iii) Reports are generally used to show the data in .... form. [1]

     (a) printed   (b) chart

     (c) Both (a) and (b)   (d) None of these

Ans. (a) printed

(iv) .... is an example of a text-based browser which provides access to the Internet in the text-only mode. [1]

    (a) Mozilla Firefox   (b) Lynx

    (c) Internet Explorer   (d) All of these

Ans. (b) Lynx

(v) Anila works in a Multi National Company (MNC) and needs to work online from home also. She requires fast Internet connection. Which type of Internet connection in your view would be best suited for her? [1]

    (a) Dialup   (b) Broadband   (c) Both are suitable   (d) None of these

Ans. (b) Broadband

(vi) Manya has created a spreadsheet using Calc, to find the average of the values in a range of cells. She wants to use a function, so that it is calculated automatically and also she can copy the same formula for other range of cells. Which of these functions will give the correct result? [1]

    (a) AVG   (b) Average

    (c) Mean   (d) None of these

Ans. (b) Average

5. Answer any 5 out of the given 6 questions   [1 × 5 = 5 Marks]

   (i) Which data type is the most appropriate to store a short bio about an employee? [1]

    (a) Text   (b) String

    (c) Memo   (d) Large text

Ans. (c) Memo

  (ii) If you have a safer and healthy workplace, there will be fewer days lost and it will have higher [1]

    (a) employee satisfaction   (b) productivity

    (c) stress levels   (d) None of these

Ans. (b) productivity

 (iii) When primary key constraint is applied on one or more columns, then it is known as [1]

    (a) composite primary key   (b) foreign key

    (c) composite foreign key   (d) connecting key

Ans. (a) composite primary key

  (iv) Naina has created a database of all the employees working in her organisation. But these entries were done randomly. Her boss wants the entire list in ascending order of employee Id. She can do this by using which of the following tools in DBMS? [1]

    (a) Ordering data   (b) Sorting data

    (c) Presenting data   (d) Referring data

Ans. (b) Sorting data

  (v) Rishabh wants to make a professional resume. He tried many a times but the end result was not satisfactory as he was not knowing what all points should be there and that too in which order . Which one of the following writer would you suggest him, so that his problem is solved?

[1]

    (a) Template   (b) Form

    (c) Worksheet   (d) Format

Ans. (a) Template

  (vi) What is the full form of RSI? [1]

    (a) Repetitive Strain Injury   (b) Rational Strain Injury

    (c) Repetitive Stress Injury   (d) Risk Strain Injury

Ans. (a) Repetitive Strain Injury

Section-B

(Subjective Type Questions)

- Answer any 3 out of the given 5 questions on Employability skills. [2 × 3 = 6 Marks]
- Answer each question in 20-30 words.

6. What are the disadvantages of non-verbal communication? [2]

Ans. Disadvantages of non-verbal communication are as follows :
- In the absence of language, this type of communication does not convey actual meaning of the message. This makes the communication imprecise.
- It can be confusing as no clear message is conveyed.
- Long conversations are not possible in non-verbal communication.
- It can be costly as Neon signs, PowerPoint presentation movies involve huge cost.

7. Write the steps to remove the password from a file. [2]

Ans. The steps to remove a password from a file are:

Click "File" and "Save As." Choose the option that saves the file with the ". "xlt" extension. Uncheck the option in the bottom left corner that says "Save with password." Press "Save".

8. How does yoga help to manage stress? [2]

Ans. Yoga is a mind-body practice that combines physical poses, controlled breathing and meditation or relaxation. It helps in stress management by relaxing the body and mind, develop a connection between them releasing emotional energy and helping to breathe more effectively.

9. What do you mean by entrepreneur? [2]

Ans. An entrepreneur is an individual who creates a new business, bearing most of the risks and enjoying most of the rewards. Entrepreneurs are innovators, who use the process of entrepreneurship to shatter the status quo of existing products and services, in order to set and new products, new services.

10. Explain any two functions of an entrepreneur. [2]

Ans. Two functions of an entrepreneur are as follows :
(i) **Innovation** It includes introducing new products, opening new markets, new sources of raw material and new organisation structure.
(ii) **Risk-taking** Choosing one among various alternatives, the end results of which are unpredictable.

- Answer any 4 out of the given 6 questions in 20-30 words each. [2 × 4 = 8 Marks]

11. How can you define OLE? [2]

Ans. **OLE objects** Use an OLE **(Object Linking and Embedding)** object to insert in a presentation either a new document or an existing one. Embedding inserts a copy of the object and details of the source program in the target document, that is the program which is associated to the file type in the operating system. The major benefit of an OLE object is that it is quick and easy to edit the contents just by double-clicking on it. You can also insert a link to the object that will appear as an icon rather than an area showing the contents itself.

12. What is the use of Consolidate option in Calc? [2]

Ans. Data > Consolidate provides a way to combine data from two or more ranges of cells into a new range while running one of the several functions (such as Sum or Average) on the data. During consolidation, the contents of cells from several sheets can be combined into one place. The effect is that copies of the identified ranges are stacked with their top left corners at the specified result position, and the selected operation is used in each cell to calculate the result value.

13. State any two ways of inserting sheets in a workbook? [2]

Ans. Two ways of inserting sheets in a workbook are as follows :
- Select **Insert > Sheet** from the Menu Bar.
- Right-click on the sheet tab and click on **Insert Sheet.**

14. How Entry Required and Default Value properties of a table field in a database are different from each other? [2]

Ans. **Entry Required** If it sets to yes then it will be necessary for the user to insert the value in the field, which means that field cannot be left blank. While **Default Value** can be set for a field, if user doesn't provide any value while making entries in the table.

15. What is Referential Integrity? Explain its purposes. [2]

Ans. Referential Integrity is a property of data stating that all its references are valid. In the context of relational databases, it is required that if a value of one attribute of a relation references a value of another attribute, then the referenced value must exist.

Referential integrity is a database concept that is used to build and maintain logical relationships between tables. It is also used to avoid logical corruption of data. It is a very useful and important part in RDBMS. Usually, referential integrity is made up of the combination of a primary key and a foreign key.

16. What is Internet Service Provider? [2]

Ans. ISP (Internet Service Provider) is a company that provides individuals and other companies access to the Internet. Internet Service Provider is used to join the Internet. Internet services typically provided by ISPs include Internet access, Internet transit, domain name registration, web hosting and usenet service. ISP does not provide E-mail address. e.g. MTNL, BSNL, Airtel etc.

- Answer any 3 out of the given 5 questions in 50-80 words each. [4 × 3 = 12 Marks]

17. Lavish is preparing notes for his upcoming exams. Help him to write the correct answer of the following: [4]

    (i) Scenario   (ii) Absolute link   (iii) Relative link   (iv) Macro

Ans. (i) The Scenario is a tool to test "What-if" questions. Each scenario is named and can be edited and formatted separately. When you print the spreadsheet, only the contents of the currently active scenario are printed.

  (ii) An absolute link contains all the information necessary to locate a resource and will stop working only if the target is moved.

 (iii) A relative link locates a resource using an absolute URL as starting point will stop working only if the start and target locations change relative to each other.

 (iv) A macro is a saved sequence of commands or keystrokes that are stored for later use or to be used repeatedly.

18. Samarjit wants to know about template. Tell him the definition of template and also the steps to create a document using it. [4]

Ans. A template is a document model that you use to create other documents. For example, you can create a template for business reports that has your company's logo on the first page. New documents created from this template will all have your company's logo on the first page. Templates can contain anything that regular documents can contain, such as text, graphics, a set of styles and user-specific setup information such as measurement units, language, the default printer, and toolbar and menu customization.

To use a template to create a document:

(i) From the main menu, choose File > New > Templates and Documents. The Templates and Documents dialog box opens.

(ii) In the box on the left, click the Templates icon if it is not already selected. A list of template folders appears in the center box.

(iii) Double-click the folder that contains the template that you want to use. A list of all the templates contained in that folder appears in the center box.

(iv) Select the template that you want to use. You can preview the selected template or view the template's properties:

 (a) To preview the template, click the Preview icon. (For the location of the Preview icon) A preview of the template appears in the box on the right.

 (b) To view the template's properties, click the Document Properties icon. (For the location of the Document Properties icon) The template's properties appear in the box on the right.

(v) Click Open. The Templates and Documents dialog box closes and a new document based on the selected template opens in Writer. You can then edit and save the new document just as you would any other document.

19. Consider the following table: SHOPPE [4]

TABLE: SHOPPE

Id	SName	Area
S001	ABC Computeronics	CP
S002	All Infotech Media	GK II
S003	Tech Shoppe	CP
S004	Geeks Tecno Soft	Nehru Place
S005	Hitech Tech Store	Nehru Place

(i) How many fields and records are there in SHOPPE table?

(ii) Write SQL commands for the following :

 (a) Display Id and SName of all the shops located in Nehru Place.

 (b) Display the details alphabetically by SName.

 (c) Display SName of shops whose Area is CP.

Ans. (i) There are 3 fields and 5 records in the table SHOPPE.

 (ii) (a) `SELECT Id, SName FROM SHOPPE WHERE Area= 'Nehru Place';`

  (b) `SELECT * FROM SHOPPE ORDER BY SName;`

  (c) `SELECT SName FROM SHOPPE WHERE Area='CP';`

20. Your friend's father owns a restaurant. He manually enters the customers records in a register. You want to explain to him the importance of creating a database in computer. Tell the advantages of using computerized database with the help of the following points: [4]

 (a) Data redundancy (b) Data inconsistency

 (c) Confidentiality (d) Sharing

Ans. (a) Data redundancy means duplication of data avoids duplication of data and ensures that there is only one instance of certain data.

 (b) Data inconsistency helps, if a single database is used by multiple users then it ensures that the same data is present for all the users.

 (c) The DBMS can ensure different views for the different users of the database. This keeps the confidentiality of the data safe.

 (d) Different users can use the same database to access the data according to their needs. Hence, DBMS provides sharing of data and resources.

21. Rahul and Amit are working on a school project assigned to them by their teacher. They have to send instant messages to each other and also do a video conferencing after school hours in order to complete the project on time. Tell the use of the following devices used for video conferencing. [4]

 (a) Microphone (b) Web camera (c) Speakers (d) Headsets

Ans. (a) Using microphone, the speaker can convey their messages.

 (b) Web camera is used to have a real-life image of the person.

 (c) Speakers are used to listen to the words of the speaker.

 (d) Headsets are used to listen to the speaker without disturbing anyone nearby.

SAMPLE QUESTION PAPER 2

Information Technology

Time : **2 hrs**   Max. Marks : **50**

Instructions

1. Please read the instructions carefully
2. This Question Paper consists of 21 questions in two sections: Section A & Section B.
3. Section A has Objective type questions whereas Section B contains Subjective type questions.
4. Out of the given (5 + 16 =) 21 questions, a candidate has to answer (5 + 10 =) 15 questions in the allotted (maximum) time of 2 hours.
5. All questions of a particular section must be attempted in the correct order.
6. Section A : Objective Type Questions (24 Marks)
   (i) This section has 05 questions.
   (ii) Marks allotted are mentioned against each question/part.
   (iii) There is no negative marking.
   (iv) Do as per the instructions given.
7. Section B: Subjective Type Questions (26 Marks)
   (i) This section has 16 questions.
   (ii) A candidate has to do 10 questions.
   (iii) Do as per the instructions given.
   (iv) Marks allotted are mentioned against each question/part.

Section-A

(Objective Type Questions)

1. Answer any 4 out of the given 6 questions based on Employability Skills   [1 × 4 = 4 Marks]

   (i) A .... is a group of sentences dealing with a particular topic.   [1]
     (a) value   (b) word
     (c) paragraph   (d) None of these
  Ans. (c) paragraph

(ii) In .... , we change from our normal activities to silence. [1]

    (a) meditation   (b) stress

    (c) worries   (d) survival

Ans. (a) meditation

(iii) .... is a common response to danger in all people and animals. [1]

    (a) Internal stress   (b) Environmental stress

    (c) Survival stress   (d) Fatigue related stress

Ans. (c) Survival stress

(iv) .... is the arrangement of elements on the slide with which the slide is available. [1]

    (a) Slide transition   (b) Slide layout

    (c) Custom animation   (d) None of these

Ans. (b) Slide layout

(v) The idea of sustainable development gained wide acceptance due to environment concerns in the .... [1]

    (a) 19th century   (b) 20th century

    (c) 21th century   (d) 18th century

Ans. (b) 20th century

(vi) There is no .... income available to an entrepreneur. [1]

    (a) leadership   (b) motivator

    (c) regular or fixed   (d) None of these

Ans. (c) regular or fixed

2. Answer any 5 out of the given 6 questions   [1 × 5 = 5 Marks]

(i) Safari is a web browser developed by .... [1]

    (a) Google   (b) Microsoft

    (c) Apple   (d) None of these

Ans. (c) Apple

(ii) When you define a field for a table, in which of the following parameters do access always considered optional? [1]

    (a) Field name   (b) Data type   (c) Field size   (d) Description

Ans. (d) Description

(iii) A ...... is a language that enables users to access and manipulate data in a database. [1]

    (a) DML   (b)DCL   (c) TCL   (d)DDL

Ans. (a) DML

(iv) To copy a formula from one cell to another. [1]

    (a) Drag the autofill handle   (b) Cut the cell

    (c) Both (a) and (b)   (d) None of these

Ans. (a) Drag the autofill handle

(v) When you apply a .... , you apply a group of formatting effects together in one single step. [1]

    (a) effect   (b) template   (c) style   (d) format

Ans. (c) style

(vi) Akshat wants to store a huge amount of information about his firm in a database. Which type of table organisation would be most suitable for this purpose? [1]

    (a) Relational   (b) Flat file

    (c) Either relational or flat file   (d) Hierarchical

Ans. (c) Either relational or flat file

3. Answer any 5 out of the given 6 questions　　　　　　　　　　　　　　　[1 × 5 = 5 Marks]

(i) Select .... > Track changes > Record from the menu bar. Thereafter, every change you record on the spreadsheet will have a red border around it.　　　[1]

(a) File　　　　　　　　　　　　　　　(b) Edit
(c) Format　　　　　　　　　　　　　(d) Layout

Ans. (b) Edit

(ii) Calc considers any data that it does not recognise as a number, date, time or formula, as:　[1]

(a) Expression　　　　　　　　　　　(b) Equation
(c) Text　　　　　　　　　　　　　　(d) Function

Ans. (c) Text

(iii) In ...... topology, each node is connected to two and only two neighbouring nodes.　　　[1]

(a) star　　　　　　　　　　　　　　(b) ring
(c) mesh　　　　　　　　　　　　　(d) tree

Ans. (b) ring

(iv) State True or False.

'Goal seek in Calc, helps us to find the desired result by adjusting an input value.'　　　[1]

(a) True　　　　　　　　　　　　　(b) False

Ans. (a) True

(v) Rajiv was asked to highlight the cells with green colour where the value entered is either greater than or equals to 120 in the worksheet containing thousands of data entries. Which feature of Calc should he use to get this work done within seconds?　　　[1]

(a) Conditional formatting　　　　　(b) Filtering
(c) Sorting　　　　　　　　　　　　(d) Simple formatting

Ans. (a) Conditional formatting

(vi) Which of the following tools will help Swati, if she wants to arrange the height of students in her class in ascending order ?　　　[1]

(a) Ordering data　　　　　　　　　(b) Sorting data
(c) Presenting data　　　　　　　　(d) Referring data

Ans. (b) Sorting data

4. Answer any 5 out of the given 6 questions　　　　　　　　　　　　　　　[1 × 5 = 5 Marks]

(i) In URL, http : // www. arihant. com/ index. htm, which component identifies the path of a web page?　　　[1]

(a) http　　　　　　　　　　　　　(b) www.arihant.com
(c) /index. htm　　　　　　　　　　(d) All of these

Ans. (c) /index. htm

(ii) What dialog box opens on choosing File > Templates > Manage Templates in Writer?　[1]

(a) The File dialog box　　　　　　　(b) The Manage Templates dialog box
(c) The Templates dialog box　　　　(d) The Record Template dialog box

Ans. (c) The Templates dialog box

(iii) .... are the ways to produce the data stored in databases and tables in a printed form.[1]

(a) Forms　　　　　　　　　　　　(b) Queries
(c) Reports　　　　　　　　　　　(d) Data

Ans. (c) Reports

(iv) Arnab learnt about a software which gets installed on the computer without the user's knowledge. Help him to find the name of the same. [1]
(a) Spyware
(b) Malware
(c) Adware
(d) None of these

Ans. (a) Spyware

(v) Tamanna wants to know the name of the kind of software which seems useful in the beginning, but will cause damage to the computer once installed. What is such kind of software called? [1]
(a) Trojan horse
(b) Worm
(c) Malware
(d) Virus

Ans. (a) Trojan Horse

(vi) .... are pre-defined formulas in Calc. [1]
(a) Functions
(b) Autofill
(c) Solver
(d) Subtotal

Ans. (a) Functions

5. Answer any 5 out of the given 6 questions   [1 × 5 = 5 Marks]

(i) If the two departments (HR and IT) access the data simultaneously then only one department will see the updates by the other department. DBMS solves this issue. Thus, DBMS helps to avoid............... which means if a single database is used by multiple users then it also ensures that the same data is present for all the users. [1]
(a) Data redundancy
(b) Data inconsistency
(c) Data piracy
(d) Data modification

Ans. (b) Data inconsistency

(ii) A .... is a set of instructions used to perform a specific task or operations. [1]
(a) Software
(b) Hardware
(c) Spyware
(d) Firewall

Ans. (a) Software

(iii) Rinky wants to know about the Number data type in Calc. Which of the following statement(s) is/are TRUE about it? [1]
(a) Numbers are generally raw numbers or dates.
(b) Numbers can be started with a dollar sign ($) or with some other currency symbols to display as currency.
(c) By default, number and date data is aligned to the right in Calc.
(d) All of the above

Ans. (d) All of the above

(iv) How much space does the DATE / TIME data type hold in Base? [1]
(a) 2 bytes
(b) 4 bytes
(c) 8 bytes
(d) 10 bytes

Ans. (c) 8 bytes

(v) Which tab is used to create Table of Contents in a document? [1]
(a) File tab
(b) Format tab
(c) Insert tab
(d) Styles tab

Ans. (c) Insert tab

(vi) ___________ is a form of electronic commerce that allows customers to directly buy goods or services from a seller on the Internet. [1]
(a) E-Shopping
(b) E-ticketing
(c) E-buying
(d) E-Delivery

Ans. (a) E-Shopping

Section-B

(Subjective Type Questions)

- Answer any 3 out of the given 5 questions on Employability skills.   [2 × 3 = 6 Marks]
- Answer each question in 20-30 words.

6. What is the role of a channel in communication cycle?   [2]

Ans. The medium or channel is the means by which a message is sent. Some messages are more effective in written form, others may be more effective on the telephone (e.g. urgent messages), while others may be more effective if sent via electronic means such as E-mail. Communication channels have noise. Noise introduced by a communication medium is anything that interferes with communication. It may cause misunderstanding of the message or even disrupt the message completely so that it is not even received.

7. How physical exercise helps in management of stress?   [2]

Ans. Physical exercise is an activity done to achieve physical fitness and overall health. It improves blood circulation, lower blood pressure, clear the mind of worrying thoughts, improves our self-image, makes us feel better about ourselves and increases social contact. It also has some direct stress-busting benefits which pumps up endorphins the chemicals in the brain that act as a natural pain killers. It also improves the ability to sleep which in turn reduces stress.

8. Explain the presentation software in brief.   [2]

Ans. Presentation software is important for school, college or office purposes. It can animate all the elements that are a part of a slide, like the text, pictures, figures, shapes, smart art etc. Apart from this, we may perform transition from slide-to-slide, with special effects as it is the part of the software. There are some presentation softwares available and these include OpenOffice Impress, Keynote, Corel Presentations, SoftMaker Presentations.

9. Describe the following characteristics of entrepreneur: [2]

    (i) Leadership   (ii) Risk Taking

Ans. (i) **Leadership** An entrepreneur must possess the characteristics of leadership and must lead a team for achievement of goals. The leader is able to clearly articulate their ideas and has a clear vision. An entrepreneurial leader realises the importance of initiative and reactiveness and go out of their way to provide a support to the team.

    (ii) **Risk Taking** An entrepreneur with rational planning and firm decisions bear the risks. They have differentiated approach towards risks. Good entrepreneurs are always ready to invest their time and money but they always have a back up for every risk they take.

10. The most significant environment problems are related to which type of resources?   [2]

Ans. The most significant environmental problems are associated with resources that are renewable such as air and water. They have a finite capacity to assimilate emissions and wastes but if pollution exceeds this capacity of ecosystem will deteriorate rapidly at a huge pace.

- Answer any 4 out of the given 6 questions in 20-30 words each.   [2 × 4 = 8 Marks]

11. What do you mean by template?   [2]

Ans A template is a collection of styles that already has some formatting in place, such as fonts, logos and line spacing and can be used as a starting point for almost anything that you want to create. Microsoft Word offers hundreds of free templates, including invoices, resumes, invitations and form letters, among others.

12. What is the difference between absolute and relative hyperlinks as used in Calc?   [2]

Ans. Hyperlinks can be stored within your file as either relative or absolute. An absolute link will stop working only if the target is moved. A relative link will stop working only if the start and target locations change relative to each other. For instance, if you have two spreadsheets in the same folder linked to each other and you move the entire folder to a new location, a relative hyperlink will not break but an absolute link will break.

13. Explain the significance of primary and foreign keys. [2]

Ans. A field which uniquely identifies each record in a table known as primary key. It does not allow null values whereas a foreign key is used to establish relationship between RDBMS.

14. Write the steps to insert a record in a Datasheet View. [2]

Ans. Steps to insert a record in a Datasheet View are as follows:
- **Step 1** When you create a table, a new blank record automatically appears in the second row of the table.
- **Step 2** If you enter data in the last record, a new blank record will automatically appear at the end of the table.
- **Step 3** Type data into the fields.
- **Step 4** When you have finished adding records in the datasheet, save it and close it.

15. Elucidate the following terms: [2]
   (i) PAN   (ii) WiMAX

Ans. (i) **PAN** It stands for Personal Area Network. It is a computer network used for communication among the computer and different technological devices close to it.
   (ii) **WiMAX** It stands for Worldwide Interoperability for Microwave Access. It is a wireless transmission of data using a variety of transmission modes.

16. State any two practices for internet security. [2]

Ans. Any two practices for internet security are:
   (i) **Use Strong Passwords** A strong password is a combination of alpha-numeric and special characters. Do not use your mobile number, friends name, etc. for a password. Change your password frequently at least once in 2 or 3 weeks.
   (ii) **Backup Your Data** Always keep copies of your personal data in CDs, pendrive, etc. This may be helpful in a loss of data situation.

- Answer any 3 out of the given 5 questions in 50-80 words each. [4 × 3 = 12 Marks]

17. Rita is working in spreadsheet. She wants to know about the use of the following terms: [4]
   (a) Quick Sort   (b) Filtering Data

Ans. (a) Quick Sort is especially useful when you add new information to a spreadsheet. When a spreadsheet is long, it is usually easier to add new information at the bottom of the sheet, rather than adding it in its correct place. After you have added information, you can sort the records to update the spreadsheet and put the information in its correct place in quick sort.
   (b) When a sheet contains a large amount of data, it can be difficult to find information quickly. In that case, Filters can be used to narrow down the data in your worksheet, allowing you to view only the information you need. In other words Filters help you to ask questions to your data and retrieve only the relevant information filtering away the un-desirable data.

18. Riddhima wants to know about mailing labels in word processor. Help her to find the answers of the given questions. [4]
   (a) What is a mailing label?
   (b) What are the ways to prepare and print mailing labels?

Ans. (a) Mailing labels are usually pieces of paper with adhesive on the back that can be affixed to packages or envelopes to identify the name and address of a recipient. They may also indicate the name and address of the person sending the mail. Mailing labels are extremely useful and time saving for the people who must send out a large volume of mail.
   (b) Mailing labels can be created in two ways:
     (i) Printing multiple copies of a single label
     (ii) Printing address lists where each label contains a different address

19. Consider the following table PRODUCT   [4]

TABLE: PRODUCT

S_NO	P_Name	S_Name	Qty	Cost	City
S1	Biscuit	Priyagold	120	12.00	Delhi
S2	Bread	Britannia	200	25.00	Mumbai
S3	Chocolate	Cadbury	350	40.00	Mumbai
S4	Sauce	Kissan	400	45.00	Chennai

(i) How many fields and records are there in PRODUCT table?

(ii) Write SQL queries for the following:

  (a) Display all Products whose Qty is between 100 and 400.

  (b) Display S_Name, P_Name, Cost for all the Products whose Qty is less than 300.

  (c) Display all the records alphabetically by S_Name.

Ans. (i) There are 6 fields and 4 records in the table PRODUCT.

  (ii) (a) `SELECT* FROM PRODUCT WHERE Qty BETWEEN 100 AND 400;`

    (b) `ELECT S _Name, P _Name, Cost FROM PRODUCT WHERE Qty <300;`

    (c) `SELECT * FROM PRODUCT  ORDER BY S_Name;`

20. Shubham is learning about DBMS. He wants to know about the following: [4]

  (a) The purpose of DBMS

  (b) Any two uses of DBMS

Ans. (a) DBMS (Database Management System) is used to store logically related information at a centralised location. It facilitates data sharing among all the applications requiring it.

  (b) Two uses of database management system are as follows :

    (i) DBMS is used to store data at a centralised location.

    (ii) It is used to minimise data redundancy and data inconsistency.

21. Rahul has purchased some stationary items from an online site. He has to make online payment for the items to complete the transaction. Help him by answering the following queries :   [4]

  (i) Suggest any two options that he can use to make payment of his bill on the online shopping website.

  (ii) Name any 2 situations where online shopping could be useful.

  (iii) Name any 2 popular online shopping websites.

  (iv) Write full form of COD in reference to online shopping.

Ans. (i) Credit, debit card or by Internet banking, etc are the options that he can use to make payment of his bill on the online shopping website.

  (ii) (a) They offer huge discount on goods and services.

    (b) Online shopping saves time and efforts in order to buy product of one's choice.

  (iii) Flipkart, Amazon are two popular online shopping websites.

  (iv) COD stands for Cash On Delivery. Cash on delivery is the sale of goods by mail order where payment is made at the time of delivery rather than in advance.

SAMPLE QUESTION PAPER 3

Information Technology

Time : **2 hrs**   Max. Marks : **50**

Instructions

1. Please read the instructions carefully
2. This Question Paper consists of 21 questions in two sections: Section A & Section B.
3. Section A has Objective type questions whereas Section B contains Subjective type questions.
4. Out of the given (5 + 16 =) 21 questions, a candidate has to answer (5 + 10 =) 15 questions in the allotted (maximum) time of 2 hours.
5. All questions of a particular section must be attempted in the correct order.
6. Section A : Objective Type Questions (24 Marks)
    (i) This section has 05 questions.
    (ii) Marks allotted are mentioned against each question/part.
    (iii) There is no negative marking.
    (iv) Do as per the instructions given.
7. Section B: Subjective Type Questions (26 Marks)
    (i) This section has 16 questions.
    (ii) A candidate has to do 10 questions.
    (iii) Do as per the instructions given.
    (iv) Marks allotted are mentioned against each question/part.

Section-A

(Objective Type Questions)

1. Answer any 4 out of the given 6 questions based on Employability Skills   [1 × 4 = 4 Marks]

(i) Which of the following is the person or organisation to whom a message is sent to?   [1]

    (a) Sender   (b) Receiver

    (c) Message   (d) None of these

Ans. (b) Receiver

(ii) Which term refers to our knowledge and understanding of ourselves? [1]
   (a) Self-awareness   (b) Motivation
   (c) Both (a) and (b)   (d) None of these

Ans. (a) Self-awareness

(iii) The ________________operating system was developed by Nokia for certain models of smartphones. [1]
   (a) Android   (b) iOS
   (c) Symbian   (d) BOSS

Ans. (c) Symbian

(iv) .... shortcut key is used to add new slides in presentation. [1]
   (a) Alt+M   (b) Ctrl+M
   (c) Ctrl+ N   (d) None of these

Ans. (b) Ctrl + M

(v) .... is a set of activities performed by the entrepreneur. [1]
   (a) Leadership   (b) Risk taking
   (c) Entrepreneurship   (d) None of these

Ans. (c) Entrepreneurship

(vi) The government should make policies against .... activities. [1]
   (a) illegal   (b) legal
   (c) Both (a) and (b)   (d) None of these

Ans. (a) illegal

2. Answer any 5 out of the given 6 questions   [1 × 5 = 5 Marks]

(i) A ...... is a temporary connection that uses the Public Switched Telephone Network (PSTN) to connect to the Internet. [1]
   (a) broadband connection   (b) wireless connection
   (c) dial-up connection   (d) None of these

Ans. (c) dial-up connection

(ii) The small area network created around a bluetooth device is called......... . [1]
   (a) LAN   (b) PAN   (c) WAN   (d) MAN

Ans. (b) PAN

(iii) The .... SQL statement is used to make a query or retrieve data from a table in a database. [1]
   (a) INSERT   (b) UPDATE
   (c) SELECT   (d) REVIEW

Ans. (c) SELECT

(iv) Which of the following allows you to reorder data? [1]
   (a) Sorting   (b) Filtering
   (c) Scenario   (d) Custom sorting

Ans. (a) Sorting

(v) Which of the following is not an AutoShape? [1]
   (a) Line   (b) Circle   (c) Curve   (d) ClipArt

Ans. (d) ClipArt

(vi) ...... is an inquiry into the database made using the SELECT statement. [1]
   (a) Query   (b) Data
   (c) Equation   (d) None of these

Ans. (a) Query

3. Answer any 5 out of the given 6 questions   [1 × 5 = 5 Marks]

(i) Editing Custom Shapes feature allows ...... of small segments of a drawing.   [1]

(a) shaping   (b) reshaping   (c) rehearse   (d) None of these

Ans. (b) reshaping

(ii) DBMS is a program, that controls the creation, maintenance and use of a database. Here, DBMS stands for   [1]

(a) Digital Base Management System   (b) Data Build Management System

(c) Database Management System   (d) Database Management Service

Ans. (c) Database Management System

(iii) A ...... filters data traffic at a network boundary.   [1]

(a) bridge   (b) switch   (c) gateway   (d) hub

Ans. (a) bridge

(iv) Template includes a text space that is surrounded by brackets. It is called a ....   [1]

(a) margin   (b) placeholder

(c) data source   (d) track changes

Ans. (b) placeholder

(v) Key field is a unique identifier for each record. It is defined in the form of _________.   [1]

(a) rows   (b) columns

(c) tree   (d) query

Ans. (b) columns

(vi) What is the name given to a combination of two cell references?   [1]

(a) Relative reference   (b) Absolute reference

(c) Mixed reference   (d) None of these

Ans. (c) Mixed reference

4. Answer any 5 out of the given 6 questions   [1 × 5 = 5 Marks]

(i) Which of the following is an application program that is stored on a remote server and delivered over the Internet?   [1]

(a) Web application   (b) System application

(c) Internet application   (d) None of these

Ans. (a) Web application

(ii) A _____________________ is a document model that you use to create other documents.   [1]

(a) Anchoring   (b) Alignment

(c) Template   (d) None of these

Ans. (c) Template

(iii) 1:1, 1:n and n:1 are examples of different types of _____________.   [1]

(a) Relations   (b) Databases   (c) Data   (d) Query

Ans. (a) Relations

(iv) In packet based networks, the message gets broken into small ....   [1]

(a) data packets   (b) data frame   (c) chunk   (d) None of these

Ans. (a) data packets

(v) Shubham wants to know the name of the function which is used to find the maximum number among the different values. Solve his query.   [1]

(a) MAX( )   (b) MAXIMISE( )

(c) MAXIMUM( )   (d) GREATER( )

Ans. (a) MAX( )

(vi) Which of the following allows you to display the specific data? [1]

    (a) Arranging   (b) Filtering

    (c) Scenario   (d) Custom sorting

Ans. (b) Filtering

5. Answer any 5 out of the given 6 questions   [1 × 5 = 5 Marks]

  (i) Which of the following is a single piece of data? [1]

    (a) Field   (b) Table   (c) Record   (d) Form

Ans. (a) Field

  (ii) URL is the .... for a website or a web page. [1]

    (a) web address   (b) website

    (c) web page   (d) Both (a) and (c)

Ans. (a) web address

(iii) Rajiv has created an employee table and made Emp_No, as the primary key, so that it can accept only unique values for each record. At the same time, he wants to have one more field that can behave like a primary key. Which of the following types of key can serve the purpose? [1]

    (a) Foreign key   (b) Candidate key

    (c) Unique key   (d) None of these

Ans. (b) Candidate key

(iv) _____________is used to define the structure of your tables and other objects in the database. [1]

    (a) DDL   (b) DML   (c) DCL   (d) None of these

Ans. (a) DDL

  (v) Suraj wants to know the sequence of steps used to open the Templates dialog. Answer to his query. [1]

    (a) File> New> Text Document   (b) File> New> Templates

    (c) Format> Group > Group   (d) None of these

Ans. (b) File> New> Templates

(vi) A .... is a series of computers linked together to form a network in a circumscribed location. [1]

    (a) LAN   (b) MAN   (c) TAN   (d) WAN

Ans. (a) LAN

Section-B

(Subjective Type Questions)

- Answer any 3 out of the given 5 questions on Employability skills.   [2 × 3 = 6 Marks]
- Answer each question in 20-30 words.

6. List the advantages of verbal communication. [2]

Ans. Some advantages of verbal communication are as follows:

- It is quick in obtaining feedback once delivered.
- It saves time in communication.
- It is a more reliable method of communication.
- It is a cheaper way of communication and, hence saves money.
- It provides complete understanding of communication delivered and there is a chance to make it more clear in case of doubts in interpretation of words or ideas.

7. How meditation can help in managing stress? [2]

Ans. In meditation, we change from our normal active state to a more peaceful state. We go beyond the noisy thoughts in the mind and enter a state of restful alertness. During meditation, although we are in a state of deep rest, our mind is fully alert and awake. At this time, the body experiences many healing effects which are the reverse of the 'fight-or-flight' response, such as decreased heart rate, normalisation of blood pressure, deeper breathing, reduced production of stress hormones, higher immunity, more efficient use of oxygen by the body and reduced inflammation.

8. Write the steps to protect the workbook with password. [2]

Ans. Protection of a Sheet To write-protect all of the cells of a sheet, you have to do the following:

- Select Tools-Protect Document from the Menu Bar, if you choose Sheet, only your current sheet will be protected from writing,
- If you choose Document, your whole document (workbook) will be protected.
- You are not obliged to enter a password, you can simply click on the OK button to close the dialog window without typing anything.
- However, if you choose a password, it will be requested every time you wish to modify the cells or the sheet.
- To eliminate the protection, choose Tools-Protect Document again and deselect the Sheet or Document option, eventually typing the password you have set, when requested.

9. How entrepreneur is helpful in capital formation? [2]

Ans. An entrepreneur is helpful in capital formation as we know that increase in the rate of capital formation is quite essential for the economic development of any country. Those nations which are not able to increase the rate of capital formation or does it nominally remain backward from industrial development's point of view.

10. How sustainable development is important to develop the positive attitude? [2]

Ans. Sustainable development brings about changes in people's knowledge, attitude and skills. It awares people about the responsibility to use and preserve natural resources. It creates the feeling that natural resources are the common property of all and nobody can use the property according to his personal will. It helps to conserve natural and social environment.

- Answer any 4 out of the given 6 questions in 20-30 words each. [2 × 4 = 8 Marks]

11. What is the use of grouping objects in a word processor application? [2]

Ans. Grouping drawing objects makes it easier to handle serveral objects as a single entity, while preserving their relative sizes and positions. When objects are grouped, any editing operations carried out on that group are pllied to all members of the group. If you click on one member of the group, the whole group is selected.

12. Write the steps for text-fitting in Word document. [2]

Ans. There are several text fitting/wrapping options in Open Office Writer.

On the main menu, click Format> Wrap. The Wrap menu options provide several possibilities:
- Alternate paragraphs and graphics, maintaining a separation between them (Wrap Off).
- Wrap text around the graphics (Page Wrap or Optimal Page Wrap).
- Put a semi-transparent graphic over the text (Wrap Through).
- Add a graphic in the background (In Background).

Often you need to insert graphics with no text around them. To set the position of an image to the Wrap Off format, follow the following steps:
(i) Select a graphic by clicking on it.
(ii) Right-click to display the context menu and move the mouse pointer to Wrap to display the various wrap modes.
(iii) Select No Wrap.
(iv) When formatting some documents, such as newsletters, you may want to put photos mixed with text or just want to add some decorative images. The Page Wrap option may satisfy this need.

(v) When an image is inserted with the Page Wrap option, you can move it anywhere on the page. The text will be automatically adjusted around the image, like water around a sailing boat.

(vi) The Optimal Page Wrap option is similar to Page Wrap, but it maintains the text positioned beside the image. The position is decided automatically in order to optimize the relative position between text and image.

The Wrap Through option lets you also insert an image overlapping the text. In this case, some part of the text will be hidden, unless you change the transparency of the image.

13. What is the use of Scenario tool? [2]

Ans. A Scenario is a set of values that Calc saves for a group of cells. Whenever we run a scenario, Calc automatically substitutes the saved cell values into a connected formula to give us an output. By having different scenarios for a same group of cells we can get different results from the formula and compare these results to know which is the most suitable set of values for us.

14. Define data, the major component of a database. [2]

Ans. Data is raw numbers, characters or facts represented by a value. Most of the organisations generate, store and process large amounts of data. The data acts as a bridge between the hardware and the software. Data may be of different types such as User data, Metadata and Application Metadata.

15. Name any two ways of wireless connections of Internet. Ramya wants to connect all the computers of her office wirelessly in order to avoid uncoordinated cables. Which wireless technology would be best suitable for her office? [2]

Ans. Wi-Fi and WiMax are the two ways of wireless connections of Internet. Wi-Fi technology would be best suitable for her office to avoid cabling. Because, it allows high speed Internet connections without the use of cables or wires.

16. What are the benefits of online shopping? [2]

Ans. Some benefits of online shopping are as follows:
- Online shopping is very convenient. You can get products at home.
- Online shopping websites provide million of choices of product.
- They offer huge discounts on goods and services.
- Online shops give us the opportunity to shop 24 x 7 and also reward us with cashback.
- Sending gifts to relatives and friends is easy by online shop.

- Answer any 3 out of the given 5 questions in 50-80 words each. [4 × 3 = 12 Marks]

17. What is sorting? How to use ascending or descending sort which depends on one column? [4]

Ans. Sorting is a common spreadsheet task that allows user to easily re-order the data. The most common type of sorting is alphabetical ordering which you can do in ascending or descending order.

To use ascending or descending sort which depends on one column, follow the given steps:

Highlight the cells to be sorted, then select Data > Sort to open the Sort dialog, or click the Sort Ascending or Sort Descending toolbar buttons. Using the dialog, you can sort the selected cells using up to three columns, in either ascending (A-Z, 1-9) or descending (Z-A, 9-1) order.

18. Shaurya had already created a paragraph style. Now, he wants to delete it. What are the steps required to delete the created style? [4]

Ans. To delete the unwanted style, Shaurya has to right-click on it in the Styles and Formatting window and choose Delete on the pop-up menu. He has to confirm deleting the style by choosing yes on the pop-up.

19. Consider the following table: Employee [4]

Table : Employee

Emp_no	E_name	Profile	Manager	Hire_date	Salary	Commission	Dept_no
8369	SMITH	CLERK	8902	1990-12-18	8000	NULL	20
8499	ANYA	SALESMAN	8698	1991-02-20	16000	300.00	30
8521	SETH	SALESMAN	8698	1991-02-22	12500	500.00	30
8566	MAHADEVAN	MANAGER	8839	1991-04-02	29850	NULL	20
8654	MOMIN	SALESMAN	8698	1991-09-28	12500	1400.00	30
8698	BINA	MANAGER	8839	1991-05-01	28500	NULL	30

(a) How many fields and records are there in the table Employee?

(b) Write the SQL queries for the following:

   (i) Display E name and Salary of those employees whose Salary is greater than or equal to 22000.

   (ii) Display details of employees those are not getting Commission.

   (iii) Display all the details of the employee profile 'SALESMAN'.

Ans. (a) There are 8 fields and 6 records in the table Employee.

  (b) (i) SELECT E_name, Salary FROM Employee WHERE Salary> = 22000;

    (ii) SELECT* FROM Employee WHERE Commission IS NULL;

    (iii) SELECT *FROM EMPLOYEE WHERE Profile="SALESMAN';

20. Define the following types of integrity : [4]

  (i) Entity integrity   (ii) Domain integrity

  (iii) Referential integrity   (iv) User defined integrity

Ans. (i) **Entity Integrity** It defines the primary key of a table. Entity integrity rule on a column does not allow duplicate and null values.

  (ii) **Domain Integrity** It defines the type, range and format of data allowed in a column. Domain integrity states that all values in a column must be of same type.

  (iii) **Referential Integrity** It defines the foreign key concepts. Referential integrity ensures that data in related tables remains accurate and consistent before and after changes.

  (iv) **User Defined Integrity** If there are some business requirements which do not fit any above data integrity then user can create own integrity, which is called user defined integrity.

21. Pinky had heard about the words types of networks. She had some doubts. Answer to her queries to clear her doubts. [4]

  (i) What is PAN?   (ii) Define the term WAN.

  (iii) Define the term MAN.   (iv) Write a disadvantage of both LAN and WAN.

Ans. (i) A Personal Area Network (PAN) is a computer network for interconnecting electronic devices within an individual person's workspace.

  (ii) A Wide Area Network (WAN) is the one which covers a broad area. It consists of two or more local area networks. A WAN is used by government organisations and businesses.

  (iii) A Metropolitan Area Network (MAN) is a computer network in which two or more computers which are geographically distributed but in the same metropolitan city are connected.

    Its geographic scope falls between a WAN and LAN.

  (iv) Disadvantage of LAN: Even though LAN saves a lot of money in terms of resource sharing, the initial cost involved in setting up the network is quite high.

    Disadvantage of WAN: It is difficult to maintain the WAN network. It requires skilled technicians and network administrators.

SAMPLE QUESTION PAPER 4

Information Technology

Time : **2 hrs**   Max. Marks : **50**

Instructions

1. Please read the instructions carefully
2. This Question Paper consists of 21 questions in two sections: Section A & Section B.
3. Section A has Objective type questions whereas Section B contains Subjective type questions.
4. Out of the given (5 + 16 =) 21 questions, a candidate has to answer (5 + 10 =) 15 questions in the allotted (maximum) time of 2 hours.
5. All questions of a particular section must be attempted in the correct order.
6. Section A : Objective Type Questions (24 Marks)
    (i) This section has 05 questions.
    (ii) Marks allotted are mentioned against each question/part.
    (iii) There is no negative marking.
    (iv) Do as per the instructions given.
7. Section B: Subjective Type Questions (26 Marks)
    (i) This section has 16 questions.
    (ii) A candidate has to do 10 questions.
    (iii) Do as per the instructions given.
    (iv) Marks allotted are mentioned against each question/part.

Section-A

(Objective Type Questions)

1. Answer any 4 out of the given 6 questions based on Employability Skills   [1 × 4 = 4 Marks]

    (i) Which of the following can make the communication difficult to be understood?   [1]

      (a) Entrepreneur   (b) Noise

      (c) Feedback   (d) Planning

  (ii) Which term means walking in the local park or a similar activity? [1]
     (a) Nature walk   (b) Motivation
     (c) Regulation   (d) None of these

 (iii) .... basically helps in arrangement of data in the correct order. [1]
     (a) Filtering   (b) Copying
     (c) Sorting   (d) Pasting

  (iv) A/An .... creates new needs and new means to satisfy them. [1]
     (a) leadership   (b) innovation
     (c) entrepreneur   (d) None of these

   (v) An entrepreneur has become the .... of modern global economy. [1]
     (a) balancing wheel   (b) goal-oriented
     (c) optimistic   (d) None of these

  (vi) Sustainable development minimises the .... of natural resources. [1]
     (a) personal attitude   (b) depletion
     (c) diversity   (d) resources

2. Answer any 5 out of the given 6 questions   [1 × 5 = 5 Marks]

   (i) .... is a form of electronic commerce where customers can buy or sell goods over the Internet. [1]
     (a) Online shopping   (b) E-Reservation
     (c) Email   (d) E-banking

  (ii) Facilities offered by databases are [1]
     (a) the ability to store a large amount of data in a structured format, easy update, sort query, production of reports.
     (b) easy edition, spell check, perform calculations, library of mathematical functions, replication.
     (c) the ability to rotate images, copy and paste, fill scale.
     (d) None of the above

 (iii) Computer based record keeping system is known as [1]
     (a) Data Manipulation System   (b) Computerised Data System
     (c) Computerised Record Keeping System (d) DBMS

  (iv) Which of the following is a spreadsheet software? [1]
     (a) Lotus 1-2-3   (b) VisiCalc
     (c) Both 'a' and 'b'   (d) None of these

   (v) A template is a model that you use to create .... [1]
     (a) images   (b) other documents
     (c) design   (d) DBMS

  (vi) Database servers are referred to as [1]
     (a) front-ends   (b) back-ends
     (c) clients   (d) model

3. Answer any 5 out of the given 6 questions   [1 × 5 = 5 Marks]

   (i) Which of the following is a set of formats consisting of such things as fonts, colors etc? [1]
     (a) Style   (b) Margin
     (c) Indent   (d) Leading

  (ii) Which of the following is not a data type? [1]
     (a) Picture/Graphic   (b) Date/Time
     (c) Text   (d) Number

(iii) .... is a Malware which is designed to spy on the victim's computer..   [1]
    (a) Virus   (b) Spyware
    (c) Worms   (d) Trojan horse

(iv) Pictures can be added to Word documents and they cannot be formatted in various ways.   [1]
    (a) True   (b) False

(v) Which function cannot be performed through Subtotal in a Spreadsheet?   [1]
    (a) Sum   (b) Product
    (c) Average   (d) Percentage

(vi) It refers to a cell or a range of cells on a worksheet and can be used to find a formula.   [1]
    (a) Row   (b) Column
    (c) Autosum   (d) Cell reference

4. Answer any 5 out of the given 6 questions   [1 × 5 = 5 Marks]

(i) A computer .... controls access between networks.   [1]
    (a) Firewall   (b) Virus
    (c) Spyware   (d) Antivirus

(ii) In a document, ... is used to apply a style to many different areas quickly without having to go back to the Styles and Formatting window and double click every time.   [1]
    (a) Fill format mode   (b) Formatting window
    (c) Painter mode   (d) Text wrapping

(iii) When you define a field for a table, ... are the names given to column in a table.   [1]
    (a) Field Name   (b) Field Size
    (c) Data Type   (d) Description

(iv) .... program(s) also offer real-time protection monitoring your computer for any changes by malware software.   [1]
    (a) Antivirus   (b) Antispyware
    (c) Both (a) and (b)   (d) None of these

(v) The ....feature creates a summarized outline of data in a worksheet.   [1]
    (a) Subtotal   (b) Solver
    (c) Goal Seek   (d) Scenario

(vi) Raj has created a worksheet where he has added all the information of his employees. He wants every employee to go through the worksheet and update their address and phone number, if required. He also would like to know the changes done by his employees. Which feature of spreadsheet he should enable to see the changes made by his employees?   [1]
    (a) Macro   (b) Link workbook
    (c) Change worksheet   (d) Track changes

5. Answer any 5 out of the given 6 questions   [1 × 5 = 5 Marks]

(i) Which of the following commands is not a Data manipulation language?   [1]
    (a) Select   (b) Insert   (c) Update   (d) Alter

(ii) The action of sharing your opinions contents on a blog is termed as ....   [1]
    (a) Blogger   (b) Blogging
    (c) Tweeting   (d) Commenting

(iii) Which data type helps you to handle an input column that is in boolean format?   [1]
    (a) OLE Object   (b) Attachment
    (c) Yes/No   (d) None of these

(iv) If you are continually working with the same range, then you may give a name to the range using .... option under Data Menu. [1]

   (a) Define data   (b) Define range

   (c) Define reference   (d) Define address

(v) In a document, ... refers to the vertical or horizontal placement of a graphic in relation to the chosen anchor point. [1]

   (a) arrangement   (b) alignment

   (c) identation   (d) margin

(vi) A .... is a location or a place of employment, where someone works to earn his living. [1]

   (a) Workplace   (b) Home

   (c) Society   (d) Industry

Section-B

(Subjective Type Questions)

- Answer any 3 out of the given 5 questions on Employability skills.   [2 × 3 = 6 Marks]
- Answer each question in 20-30 words.

6. Write the advantages of non-verbal communication. [2]

7. What do you mean by internal stress? [2]

8. What are the facilities provided by operating system? [2]

9. Explain innovativeness as a quality of entrepreneur. [2]

10. Give the short term solutions for sustainable development. [2]

- Answer any 4 out of the given 6 questions in 20-30 words each.   [2 × 4 = 8 Marks]

11. Explain the role of template in word processor? [2]

12. What is the difference between a workbook and a worksheet? [2]

13. Write down the significance of electronic spreadsheets. [2]

14. When is Memo data type is preferred over Text data type for a field? [2]

15. Write the steps to create a form using split form command. [2]

16. Define router as network device. [2]

- Answer any 3 out of the given 5 questions in 50-80 words each.   [4 × 3 = 12 Marks]

17. What is sorting? How to use ascending or descending sort which depends on one column? [4]

18. Write one example of each field for which you would use [4]

   (i) Text data type   (ii) Memo data type

19. Consider the following table: Employee   [4]

Table : Employee

Emp_no	E_name	Profile	Manager	Hire_date	Salary	Commission	Dept_no
8369	SMITH	CLERK	8902	1990-12-18	8000	NULL	20
8499	ANYA	SALESMAN	8698	1991-02-20	16000	300.00	30
8521	SETH	SALESMAN	8698	1991-02-22	12500	500.00	30
8566	MAHADEVAN	MANAGER	8839	1991-04-02	29850	NULL	20
8654	MOMIN	SALESMAN	8698	1991-09-28	12500	1400.00	30
8698	BINA	MANAGER	8839	1991-05-01	28500	NULL	30

(a) How many fields and records are there in the table Employee?

(b) Write the SQL queries for the following:

(i) Display E name and salary of those employees whose Salary is less than or equal to 16000.

(ii) Display details of employees who are getting commission of ₹ 300 or greater.

(iii) Display all the details of the employee profile 'CLERK'.

20. Ajay is learning about the different terms and commands of a database. He came across the following terms . Tell him the definition of the following   [4]

(i) Insert command   (ii) Select command

(iii) Delete command   (iv) DCL command

21. Sonia had heard about the various types of ISPs. She had some doubts. Answer to her queries to clear her doubts.   [4]

(a) What is an ISP?

(b) Name any two ISPs of India.

(c) Name any two connection types that home users use.

(d) What is satellite?

Answers

1. (i) (b) (ii) (a) (iii) (c) (iv) (c) (v) (a) (vi) (b)

2. (i) (a) (ii) (a) (iii) (d) (iv) (c) (v) (b) (vi) (b)

3. (i) (a) (ii) (a) (iii) (b) (iv) (b) (v) (d) (vi) (d)

4. (i) (a) (ii) (a) (iii) (a) (iv) (c) (v) (a) (vi) (d)

5. (i) (d) (ii) (b) (iii) (c) (iv) (b) (v)(b) (vi) (a)

6. Following are the advantages of non-verbal communication:

- It conveys clear and precise meaning to the receiver.
- It is presentable through visuals, audio-visual and silent means.
- This type of communication serves as a substitute for verbal communication.
- It is helpful in communicating with illiterate people.
- It is attractive in nature as pictures, graphs etc. attract everybody's attention.
- It is very impactful as visuals greatly affect minds of people.

7. Internal stress generates within the humans regarding unreasonable matters. This internal stress is one of the most important kinds of stress to understand and manage because it keeps on building up as time passes. For example, some people become used to the kind of hurried, tense, lifestyle of persons living in large cities. They even look for stressful situations and feel stress about matters which may not be stressful at all. This stress affects our work performance adversely. Internal stress is a result of unexpressed worries.

8. The facilities provided by operating system are:
   - Easy interaction between humans and computers.
   - Starting computer automatically when power is turned on.
   - Loading and scheduling users' programs along with necessary compilers.
   - Controlling Input and Output.

9. With the changing needs and requirements of customers production should meet requirements with the help of innovative ideas. An entrepreneurial venture does not have to restrict itself to just one innovation or even one type of innovation. Success can be built on combination of innovation for example, a new product delivered in a new way with a new message.

10. Short term solutions for sustainable development are:
    - Illegal deforestation and smuggling of forest resources should be stopped.
    - Proper balance ought to be maintained between deforestation and afforestation.
    - Planning and building of industrial zones to manage and process are types of wastes.

11. In word processor, templates are a special type of document that can hold text, styles, macros, keyboard shortcuts, custom toolbars, QAT and ribbon modifications and building blocks including Auto Text entries.

12. Differences between workbook and worksheet are as follows:

Workbook	Worksheet
A workbook is an Excel file with one or more worksheets	A worksheet is a single spreadsheet of data.
A workbook would be the entire binder, with everything in it.	A worksheet would be like one section in that binder.

13. Using electronic spreadsheets, large volume of data can be stored in worksheets. Worksheets can be managed, edited, viewed, retrieved and printed easily in desired format. Electronic spreadsheets support charts, which represent data pictorially.

14. Text data type is not capable to store the project description because its length cannot be more than 255 characters so, Memo data type is preferred over Text data type.

15. To create a form using a Split Form command, follow the given steps:
    - *Step 1* First, select the table for which you want to create a form.
    - *Step 2* Click the Create tab in the ribbon.
    - *Step 3* Select Split Form option from the Forms group.

    After this, form will be shown in the upper part and lower part will show the datasheet view.

16. Router is a network device designed to take incoming packets, analyse the packets, move the packets to another network, convert the packets to another network interface, drop the packets, direct packets to the appropriate locations, etc. A router functions similar to a bridge. However, unlike a bridge, a router passes data packets from one network to another network based on their IP addresses not MAC addresses.

17. Sorting is a common spreadsheet task that allows user to easily re-order the data. The most common type of sorting is alphabetical ordering which you can do in ascending or descending order.

    To use ascending or descending sort which depends on one column, follow the given steps:
    - Highlight the cells to be sorted, then select Data > Sort to open the Sort dialog, or click the Sort Ascending or Sort Descending toolbar buttons. Using the dialog, you can sort the selected cells using up to three columns, in either ascending (A-Z, 1-9) or descending (Z-A, 9-1) order.

18. (i) **Text data type** It allows to store text or combination of text and numbers as well as numbers that don't require calculations such as phone number. This data type allows maximum 255 characters to store. e.g. If Employee is a table and Emp_No, Name and Description are fields, then name will be a Text field. Because, Name is a character entry field.

   (ii) **Memo data type** It allows long blocks of text that uses text formatting. e.g. In the Employee table, the field Description will be of Memo data type, because the length of description of employee may be large.

19. (a) There are 8 fields and 6 records in the table Employee.

   (b) (i) SELECT E_name, Salary FROM Employee

        WHERE Salary< = 16000;

     (ii) SELECT* FROM Employee WHERE Commission >= 300;

    (iii) SELECT *FROM EMPLOYEE WHERE Profile="CLERK';

20. (i) **Insert Command** It is used to add a single record or multiple records into a table.

Syntax

```
Insert into <table_name> (col1, col2.....) values (val1, val2);
```

   (ii) **Select Command** It is used to query or retrieve data from a table in the database.

Syntax

```
Select column_list from table_name;
```

   (iii) **Delete Command** To discard unwanted data from a database, the delete command is used.

Syntax

```
Delete from <table_name> WHERE <condition>;
```

   (iv) **DCL Command** These commands are used to assign security levels in database which involves multiple user setups. They are used to grant defined role and access privileges to the users.

21. (a) An Internet Service Provider (ISP) is an organisation which provides you with access to the Internet *via* wired or wireless connection. To use the Internet, you need an Internet connection.

   (b) Internet connections are provided by the Internet Service Providers (ISPs) such as Bharat Sanchar Nigam Limited (BSNL), MTNL, Airtel, Vodafone, Reliance, Tata Indicom, etc.

   (c) The home users use cable modem(type of broadband connection) and Wi-Fi(Wireless Fidelity). It is a popular technology that allows an electronic device such as computer or mobile phone to exchange data wirelessly over a network.

   (d) Satellites orbit around the Earth and provide necessary links for telephone and television services.

SAMPLE QUESTION PAPER 5

Information Technology

Time : **2 hrs**   Max. Marks : **50**

Instructions

1. Please read the instructions carefully
2. This Question Paper consists of 21 questions in two sections: Section A & Section B.
3. Section A has Objective type questions whereas Section B contains Subjective type questions.
4. Out of the given (5 + 16 =) 21 questions, a candidate has to answer (5 + 10 =) 15 questions in the allotted (maximum) time of 2 hours.
5. All questions of a particular section must be attempted in the correct order.
6. Section A : Objective Type Questions (24 Marks)
   (i) This section has 05 questions.
   (ii) Marks allotted are mentioned against each question/part.
   (iii) There is no negative marking.
   (iv) Do as per the instructions given.
7. Section B: Subjective Type Questions (26 Marks)
   (i) This section has 16 questions.
   (ii) A candidate has to do 10 questions.
   (iii) Do as per the instructions given.
   (iv) Marks allotted are mentioned against each question/part.

Section-A

(Objective Type Questions)

1. Answer any 4 out of the given 6 questions based on Employability Skills   [1 × 4 = 4 Marks]

   (i) .... is the process in which the receiver interprets and understands the message.   [1]
       (a) Encoding   (b) Decoding   (c) Sender   (d) Receiver

   (ii) .... generates within the human regarding the unreasonable matters.   [1]
       (a) Internal stress   (b) Survival stress
       (c) Environmental stress   (d) None of these

(iii) An .... is a software program that manages the hardware and software resources of a computer. [1]

    (a) Application   (b) Operating system (OS)

    (c) System   (d) None of these

(iv) An entrepreneur must establish good relations with .. .. and its functionaries. [1]

    (a) customer   (b) government

    (c) Both (a) and (b)   (d) None of these

(v) The overall effects of economic activities on the environment are continuously........... [1]

    (a) editing   (b) changing

    (c) formatting   (d) All of these

(vi) Energy demand in developing countries will increase to .... times the current levels by 2030. [1]

    (a) four   (b) five

    (c) six   (d) eight

2. Answer any 5 out of the given 6 questions   [1 × 5 = 5 Marks]

(i) Every computer is protected by a .... [1]

    (a) firewall   (b) software

    (c) server   (d) network

(ii) The structure line displays the elements for entries in the level column. The .... button represents the page number. [1]

    (a) #   (b)   (c) %   (d)@

(iii) ...... command is used to restore database to original since the last COMMIT. [1]

    (a) REVIEW   (b) SELECT

    (c) ROLLBACK   (d) None of these

(iv) Default name of first scenario created in Sheetl of Calc is ----- [1]

    (a) Sheet_l_Scenario   (b) Sheet_Scenario_l

    (c) Sheetl_Scenario_l   (d) None of these

(v) To delete a template, ... on a template in the Templates window and select delete. [1]

    (a) Right-click   (b) Double-click

    (c) Left-click   (d) None of these

(vi) Which of the following fields will not make a suitable primary key? [1]

    (a) A customer's account number   (b) A date-field

    (c) An auto number field   (d) A student's admission number

3. Answer any 5 out of the given 6 questions   [1 × 5 = 5 Marks]

(i) Under Insert tab, ... group contains the features like Shapes, ClipArt etc. [1]

    (a) Illustrations   (b) Shapes   (c) Paragraph   (d) Clipboard

(ii) .... command is used to retrieve data from a database. [1]

    (a) SELECT   (b) INSERT

    (c) UPDATE   (d) None of these

(iii) Instant messaging service accepts instant messages from .... [1]

    (a) external sites   (b) internal sites

    (c) Both (a) and (b)   (d) None of these

(iv) Two other toolbars can be opened from Picture Tool bar are : the .... and .... [1]

    (a) Edit picture, Color picture   (b) Format, drawing

    (c) Graphic Filter toolbar, Color toolbar   (d) Floating toolbar, Color toolbar

(v) In the Subtotal dialog box, the .... box is used to select the column on which you want to add the Subtotal to. [1]

   (a) group by   (b) filter by

   (c) consolidate by   (d) update by

(vi) Commands are a set of instructions that is used to interact with database. [1]

   (a) SQL   (b) Java

   (c) Mac   (d) DBMS

4. Answer any 5 out of the given 6 questions   [1 × 5 = 5 Marks]

  (i) Type of software is accessed using browsers [1]

   (a) Open source   (b) Both (a) and (c)

   (c) Web based   (d) None of these

  (ii) Under .... tab, Bullet and Numbering, Autocorrect etc options are present. [1]

   (a) Tools   (b) Format   (c) Window   (d) Table

 (iii) ...... is a collection of related information [1]

   (a) base   (b) Database

   (c) web-base   (d) None of these

 (iv) Which of the following network devices is used to connect to dissimilar networks? [1]

   (a) Gateway   (b) Switch   (c) Bridge   (d) Router

  (v) You should uninstall any .... and services which you are not using from long time. [1]

   (a) hardware   (b) software

   (c) system   (d) None of these

 (vi) In Goal seek dialog box, the .... we enter the reference of the cell that contains the value to be changed. [1]

   (a) variable cell   (b) modifying cell

   (c) changing cell   (d) replacing cell

5. Answer any 5 out of the given 6 questions   [1 × 5 = 5 Marks]

  (i) Key field is a unique identifier for each record. It is defined in the form of [1]

   (a) rows   (b) columns

   (c) tree   (d) query

  (ii) ...... is used to text-to-speech utility that reads what is displayed on the screen. [1]

   (a) Start Narrator   (b) Web page

   (c) Website   (d) None of these

 (iii) Computer based record keeping system is known as .... [1]

   (a) Data Manipulation System   (b) Computer Data System

   (c) Computerised Record Keeping System   (d) DBMS

 (iv) The comments that are added while creating a scenario is displayed in the .... while using scenario. [1]

   (a) preview pane   (b) navigator box

   (c) comment window   (d) None of these

  (v) Which of the following is not a type of text wrapping option? [1]

   (a) Wrap off   (b) Optimal wrap

   (c) Page wrap   (d) Wrap center

 (vi) ..... is a free personal publishing platform. [1]

   (a) Zoomla   (b) WordPress

   (c) Blogger   (d) None of these

Section-B

(*Subjective Type Questions*)

- Answer any 3 out of the given 5 questions on Employability skills. [2 × 3 = 6 Marks]
- Answer each question in 20-30 words.

6. What are the disadvantages of verbal communication? [2]

7. What do you mean by environmental stress? [2]

8. Write any two main advantages of an operating system. [2]

9. Describe the following functions of an entrepreneur: [2]
  (i) Innovation   (ii) Risk-Taking

10. Explain long lasting development as an importance of sustainable development. [2]

- Answer any 4 out of the given 6 questions in 20-30 words each. [2 × 4 = 8 Marks]

11. Write some features of spelling checker in open office writer. [2]

12. Write the steps for identifying dupilcates in excel. [2]

13. What is data analysis in a spreadsheet software? [2]

14. Explain the term relational database management system. [2]

15. What do you mean by data control language? Also, give its types. [2]

16. Describe the term wireless fidelity. [2]

- Answer any 3 out of the given 5 questions in 50-80 words each. [4 × 3 = 12 Marks]

17. Simran wants to know about Subtotal. Answer the given questions for her. [4]
  (i) What is SUBTOTAL( ) function?
  (ii) Names of any 5 functions with their function index number.

18. Ram wants to compress a picture. Write the steps through which he can do so. [4]

19. Consider the following table: MASTER [4]

Table : MASTER

SNo	Name	Age	Department	Salary
1	Shyam	21	Computer	12000
2	Shiv	25	Maths	15000
3	Rakesh	31	Hindi	14000
4	Sharmila	32	History	20000
5	Dushyant	25	Software	30000

(i) How many fields and records are there in the table MASTER?

(ii) Write the SQL queries to:

(a) Display all the records according to Age.

(b) Display Name and Department of the person having salary less than 20000.

(c) Display the Name of the person having age less than 30.

20. Yuan is learning about database. But, he didn't understand the concept of field, records and table. Answer to him the following queries: [4]

(i) How are fields, record and a table related to each other? Explain with the help of an example.

(ii) What are the main purposes of a database system?

21. Reema has been appointed as SME in an IT based company. Tell her the following: [4]

(i) What is workplace emergency?

(ii) Name the workplace emergencies that may happen.

Answers

1. (i)(b), (ii)(a),(iii)(b),(iv)(b),(v)(b),(vi)(c)

2. (i)(a), (ii)(a),(iii)(c),(iv)(c),(v)(a),(vi)(b)

3. (i)(a), (ii)(a),(iii)(a),(iv)(b),(v)(a),(vi)(a)

4. (i)(c), (ii)(b),(iii)(b),(iv)(a),(v)(b),(vi)(a)

5. (i)(b), (ii)(a),(iii)(d),(iv)(b),(v)(d),(vi)(b)

6. Following are the disadvantages of verbal communication are:
- It has no legal validity and hence will lead to problems in certain situations. Emotions are visible and hence leads to trouble in certain cases.
- It has issues when communicating with distant people.
- It does not provide permanent record unless it is recorded with modern means of storage.
- This form of communication is not suitable for lengthy message.

7. Environmental stress is a response to happenings around us that cause stress, such as noise, pollution, crowding, pressure of work, family tensions etc. Some of these may be under our control if we try to control them, whereas some may not be controllable. Identifying these environmental stresses and learning to avoid them or deal with them will help lower our stress level.

8. The main advantages of an operating system include:
- Allows multiple programs to run concurrently.
- Simplifies the programming of application software because the program does not have to manage the hardware. The operating systems manages all hardware and the interaction of software. It also gives the program a high-level interface to the hardware and ways of interacting with other programs.

9. (i) **Innovation** It includes introducing new products, opening new markets, new sources of raw material and new organisation structure.

(ii) **Risk-Taking** An entrepreneur has to take risk by choosing one among various alternatives.

10. Sustainable development aims at achieving the goal of economic and social development without destroying the Earth's means and resources. It attempts to create the concept of maintaining the present work for the future and conserving the natural resources for future generation.

11. • You can right-click on a word with a wavy underline, to open a context menu. If you select from the suggested words on the menu, the selection will replace the misspelled word in your text.

 • You can change the dictionary language (for example, to Spanish, French or German) on the Spelling dialog box.

 • You can add a word to the dictionary. Click Add in the Spelling dialog box and pick the dictionary to add it to.

 • The Options dialog of the Spelling tool has a number of different options, such as whether to check uppercase words and words with numbers. It also allows you to manage custom dictionaries; that is, add or delete dictionaries, and add or delete words in a dictionary.

12. To identify duplicates :

 1. Select the cells you want to check for duplicates.

 2. Click Home > Conditional Formatting > Highlight Cells Rules > Duplicate Values.

 3. In the box next to values with, pick the formatting you want to apply to the duplicate values, and then click OK.

13. Data analysis is a process of inspecting, cleansing, transforming, and modeling data with the aim of deriving useful information from it, which can further be used in an organization's decision making process. In the previous class we have learnt to use formulas and functions for manipulation and analysis of data. Calc offers several other tools for analyzing and manipulating spreadsheets including data consolidation, subtotals, scenarios, Goal seek and Solvers etc. All these tools are organized in two menus-Tools menu and data menu.

14. RDBMS (Relational Database Management System) is a type of DBMS that stores data in the form of relations (tables). Relational databases are powerful, so they require few assumptions about how data is related or how it will be extracted from the databases.

 An important feature of relational database system is that a single database can be spread across several tables. Base, Oracle, DB2, SAP, Sybase, ASE, lnformix, Access etc. are the examples of RDBMS.

15. DCL (Data Control Language) commands are used to assign security levels in database which involves multiple user setups. They are used to grant defined role and access privileges to the users.

 Two types of DCL commands are :

 (i) GRANT Used to give user's access privileges to database.

 (ii) REVOKE Used to withdraw access privileges given with the GRANT command.

16. Wireless Fidelity (Wi-Fi) is a universal wireless networking technology that utilises radio frequencies to transfer data. Wi-Fi allows high speed Internet connections without the use of cables or wires. Wi-Fi networks can be designed for private access within a home or business. It can be used for public Internet access at 'hotspots' that offers Wi-Fi access such as restaurants, coffee shops, hotels, airports, convention centres and city parks.

17. (i) The SUBTOTAL function is listed in the mathematical category of functions. It is used to calculate subtotals for a given range with the help of another function defined within it. The general syntax of the SUBTOTAL function is as follows:

 SUBTOTAL (Function; Range)

 Here, Function is the index number for one of the following functions:

 (ii) Any 5 functions with their function index number are:

Function	Function index
Average ()	1
Count ()	2
Counta ()	3
Max ()	4
Min ()	5

18. To resize an image:

 1. Click one time on the image to select it.

 2. From the Menu bar select: Format ? Position and Size.

 3. Choose the Position & Size tab.

 4. Insert the desired image size and click the OK button.

Or

 1. Click one time on the image to select it. Little green squares will appear around the image.

 2. Drag one of the squares to resize the image.

19. (i) There are 5 fields and 5 records in the table MASTER.

    (ii) (a) SELECT * FROM MASTER ORDER BY Age;

        (b) SELECT Name, Department FROM MASTER WHERE Salary<20000;

        (c) SELECT Name FROM MASTER WHERE Age <30;

20. (i) Fields are a type of information. A record contains logically related fields. A table contains logically related records.

Table : Emp

Emp No	Name	Salary
1	Shridhar	20,000
2	Raghav	40,000

In table Emp, EmpNo, Name and Salary are three different fields. 1, Shridhar, 20,000 represents one complete record.

    (ii) The main purposes of a DBMS are

        (a) Storage of information

        (b) Retrieval of information quickly.

        (c) Sorting, selecting data that satisfies certain and readable format.

        (d) Produce the report in some standardised and readable format.

21. (i) A workplace emergency is an unforeseen situation that threatens your employees, customers, or the public; disrupts or shuts down the workplace operations; or causes physical or environmental damage.

    (ii) Emergencies may be natural or manmade and include the following:

(i) Floods,	(ii) Hurricanes,	(iii) Tornadoes,
(iv) Fires,	(v) Toxic gas releases,	(vi) Chemical spills,
(vii) Radiological accidents,	(viii) Explosions,	
(ix) Civil disturbances, and	(x) Workplace violence resulting in bodily harm and trauma.	

SAMPLE QUESTION PAPER 6

Information Technology

Time : **2 hrs**   Max. Marks : **50**

Instructions

1. Please read the instructions carefully
2. This Question Paper consists of 21 questions in two sections: Section A & Section B.
3. Section A has Objective type questions whereas Section B contains Subjective type questions.
4. Out of the given (5 + 16 =) 21 questions, a candidate has to answer (5 + 10 =) 15 questions in the allotted (maximum) time of 2 hours.
5. All questions of a particular section must be attempted in the correct order.
6. Section A : Objective Type Questions (24 Marks)
    (i) This section has 05 questions.
    (ii) Marks allotted are mentioned against each question/part.
    (iii) There is no negative marking.
    (iv) Do as per the instructions given.
7. Section B: Subjective Type Questions (26 Marks)
    (i) This section has 16 questions.
    (ii) A candidate has to do 10 questions.
    (iii) Do as per the instructions given.
    (iv) Marks allotted are mentioned against each question/part.

Section-A

(Objective Type Questions)

1. Answer any 4 out of the given 6 questions based on Employability Skills   [1 × 4 = 4 Marks]

    (i) .... is essential to complete the cycle of communication.   [1]

      (a) Encoding   (b) Decoding

      (c) Feedback   (d) Sender

(ii) The good stress is called........... .   [1]
   (a) eustress   (b) emstress
   (c) Both (a) and (b)   (d) None of these

(iii) Windows 10 is an operating system developed by ....   [1]
   (a) Microsoft™   (b)IBM   (c) Samsung   (d) Sony

(iv) How can an entrepreneur get the work done from his/her team?   [1]
   (a) By creating a spirit of teamwork   (b) By motivation
   (c) Using harsh words and actions   (d) Both (a) and (b)

(v) Sustainable development requires the judicious use of ....   [1]
   (a) resources   (b) verbal resources
   (c) natural resources   (d) None of these

(vi) If sustainable development is neglected then   [1]
   (a) we shall have a safe and secure environment.
   (b) it will destroy ecology and environment endangering the survival of future generation.
   (c) mankind will continue to live and prosper.
   (d) All of the above

2. Answer any 5 out of the given 6 questions   [1 × 5 = 5 Marks]

(i) After adding the data source, you need to specify the salutation. The selected salutation will be displayed in the pane.   [1]
   (a) salutation   (b) preview   (c) display   (d) None of these

(ii) Cell referencing can be done by using a .... as well ....   [1]
   (a) keyboard, windows menu   (b) keyboard, mouse
   (c) windows menu, mouse   (d) None of these

(iii) Full form of OLE is ....   [1]
   (a) Object Linked and Embedded   (b) Option Linking and Embedding
   (c) Open Linking and Embedding   (d) Object Linking and Embedding

(iv) We can rename a new sheet in Calc.   [1]
   (a) After inserting a new sheet   (b) While inserting a new sheet
   (c) Both (a) and (b)   (d) None of these

(v) To start the macro recorder, which of the following command is used?   [1]
   (a) Tools → Macros →Record Macro   (b) Tools →Record→Record Macro
   (c) Data→ Macros→Record   (d) None of these

(vi) In case, another user is trying to save the shared worksheet and resolve conflicts, you see a message that the shared spreadsheet file is due to a merge in progress.   [1]
   (a) stopped   (b) locked
   (c) Both (a) and (b)   (d) None of these

3. Answer any 5 out of the given 6 questions   [1 × 5 = 5 Marks]

(i) In a document, you can insert ....   [1]
   (a) Pictures   (b) ClipArts
   (c) Shapes   (d) All of these

(ii) Which of the following is not the main building block of a database?   [1]
   (a) Lists   (b) Queries   (c) Reports   (d) Forms

(iii) ....is a computer program that provides services to other computer programs.   [1]
   (a) Server   (b) Client
   (c) Network   (d) None of these

(iv) State True or False. [1]

ClipArt object includes effects such as shadows, outlines, colors, gradients and 3D effects.
(a) True   (b) False

(v) In order to group sheets, while holding the...... key , click on the Sheets tab you want to group. [1]

(a) Alt   (b) Shift   (c) Ctrl   (d) Tab

(vi) If a table has to be created which tab and group should be used? [1]
(a) Insert tab → Tables group   (b) Home tab → Tables group
(c) Design tab → Tables group   (d) None of these

4. Answer any 5 out of the given 6 questions [1 × 5 = 5 Marks]

(i) ...... is a network architecture which separates the client from the server. [1]
(a) Client Server Network   (b) Peer - to - Peer Network
(c) Both (a) and (b)   (d) None of these

(ii) In the hierarchy of headings, the lower - level headings pertain to .... and .... [1]
(a) section, sub-sections   (b) headings, sub-headings
(c) Both (a) and (b)   (d) None of these

(iii) TCL commands are used to manage ...... in database. [1]
(a) data   (b) values
(c) transactions   (d) None of these

(iv) ...... is used to begin text-to-speech utility that reads what is displayed on the screen. [1]
(a) Start Narrator   (b) Web page
(c) Website   (d) None of these

(v) ...... provides the physical connection between the network and computer workstation. [1]
(a) LIC   (b) NC
(c) NIC   (d) None of these

(vi) In Calc, you can insert the data from different databases and other data sources. One such
format is [1]
(a) odd   (b) .dbms
(c) .odb   (d) .ods

5. Answer any 5 out of the given 6 questions [1 × 5 = 5 Marks]

(i) ...... leads to data inconsistency. [1]
(a) Data integrity   (b) Data sharing
(c) Data redundancy   (d) Data recovery

(ii) Blog Desk is an offline blog editor which is used for ...... operating system. [1]
(a) Linux   (b) Unix
(c) Windows   (d) None of these

(iii) To create the link from one document to another, both the documents should be [1]
(a) open   (b) closed
(c) Both (a) and (b)   (d) None of these

(iv) Which of the following is not true? [1]
(a) More than one people can work simultaneously on a shared worksheet.
(b) Shared spreadsheet can be modified by other users.
(c) You cannot make changes in a sheet, if it is not shared with you.
(d) Other users can save the shared file while you resolving the conflicts.

(v) Suhani has written an article on 'Sustainable Development Goals' in about 1000 words. She has given appropriate headings and subheadings in it. She has also created a table of contents using the hierarchy of headings. She also wants to customize the look of the table of contents by adding an image in its background. Which of the following option under the background tab she should select to add an image? [1]

(a) Image   (b) Picture

(c) Bitmap   (d) Art

(vi) A web page is located using a [1]

(a) Universal Record Linking   (b) Universal Record Locator

(c) Uniform Resource Locator   (d) Uniformly Reachable Links

Section-B

(Subjective Type Questions)

- Answer any 3 out of the given 5 questions on Employability skills. [2 × 3 = 6 Marks]
- Answer each question in 20-30 words.

6. Describe any two types of barriers to communication in one sentence each with examples. [2]

7. Why is self-regulation important in life? [2]

8. Explain any two items of the Windows desktop. [2]

9. Explain the role and significance of entrepreneurs. [2]

10. Why is there a need for sustainable development? Give reasons. [2]

- Answer any 4 out of the given 6 questions in 20-30 words each. [2 × 4 = 8 Marks]

11. What are objects in a word processing software? [2]

12. How to insert the copyright symbol into a Word document? [2]

13. What is the use of Auto Sum in spreadsheet? [2]

14. A table named School (containing data of students of the entire school) is created, where each record consists of several fields including AdmissionNo (Admission Number), RollNo (Roll Number), Name. Which field out of these three should be set as the primary key and why? [2]

15. List any two advantages associated with networking. [2]

16. Explain the purpose of a blog. [2]

- Answer any 3 out of the given 5 questions in 50-80 words each. [4 × 3 = 12 Marks]

17. Explain the Scenario tool of a spreadsheet software. [4]

18. Ojas had prepared a Table of Contents of the project work he had done in a word processor application.

(a) Tell him the different steps to update the TOC [4]

(b) Tell him the different steps to delete the TOC

19. Consider the following table: SummerCamp. [4]

Table : SummerCamp

Child ID	First Name	Last Name	DOB	Gender	Group
109	Vedansh	Gupta	30/06/10	M	2A
214	Mack	Tyagi	09/12/08	M	1B
115	Aditi	Thakur	13/04/09	F	1A
108	Vikrant	Chauhan	02/02/09	M	2A
141	Swati	Saini	06/05/10	F	2B
233	Vishakha	Tyagi	01/08/10	F	3A
274	Madhur	Gupta	06/03/10	M	3B

(i) How many fields and records are there in the table SummerCamp?

(ii) Write SQL queries for the following:

    (a) Display all the record of table SummerCamp whose DOB is between 02/02/09 and 06/03/10.

    (b) Display all the records having Gender F.

    (c) Display all the records according to the First Name.

20. Lavish wants to know the following points about database. [4]

(a) Definition of a Database Management System.

(b) Any two advantages of using database management system for school.

21. Manya is studying about the different topologies available in networking. Tell her the difference between Star topology and Bus topology with the help of a suitable diagram. [4]

Answers

1. (i)(c), (ii)(a),(iii)(a),(iv)(d),(v)(c),(vi)(b)

2. (i)(b), (ii)(b),(iii)(d),(iv)(c),(v)(a),(vi)(b)

3. (i)(d), (ii)(a),(iii)(a),(iv)(b),(v)(c),(vi)(c)

4. (i)(a), (ii)(a),(iii)(c),(iv)(a),(v)(c),(vi)(c)

5. (i)(c), (ii)(c),(iii)(a),(iv)(d),(v)(c),(vi)(c)

6. The two types of barriers to communication are :

    (i) **Physical** These are environmental factors which prevent or reduce the sending and receiving of communications, such as physical distance, distracting noises and similar interferences.

    (ii) **Personal** These cause a psychological distance between people similar to the physical distance, as they include judgements, emotions and social values of people, which change or distort the communication.

7. Self-regulation is important in life due to the following reasons:

    (i) Self-regulation allows you to keep a tab on your own emotions.

    (ii) Self-regulation enables to develop the idea about 'what is appropriate behaviour' and 'what is inappropriate behaviour' in a given social condition.

    (iii) It helps in controlling negative impulses and reciprocate emotions for actualising set goals.

8. Any two items of the Windows desktop are:

    • Taskbar

It is present in the bottom area of the desktop. It contains Start button, Cortana, Task View button, Quick Launch Bar and Notification Area.

    • Icons

The small pictures on the desktop which represent various programs/applications are called icons.

9. The role and significance of entrepreneurs are discussed below:

- **Organiser of Society's Productive Resources** An entrepreneur is the organise of society's productive resources. He is the person who assembles the unused natural, physical and human resources of the society, combines them properly, establishes effective coordination between them and makes the economic activities dynamic.
- **Helpful in Capital Formation** An entrepreneur is helpful in capital formation as we know that increase in the rate of capital formation is quite essential for the economic development of any country.
- **Increase in Employment** Opportunities An entrepreneur creates maximum employment opportunities in the society by way of establishing new industries, developing and expanding the existing industries and by undertaking innovative activities.

10. Sustainable development is necessary for the maintenance of the environment.

There is a need of sustainable development because of the following reasons:

(i) Sustainable development teaches people to make use of means and resources for the maximum benefit without wastage.

(ii) Sustainable development brings about changes in people's knowledge, attitUde and skill.

(iii) Sustainable development aims at achieving the goal of economic and social development without destroying the Earth's means and resources.

11. The word processor object allows different formatting within the same object. However, word processor objects are printed as an image, so they require quite a bit more resources than a normal single or multiline text objects. Word processing objects includes text, graphical and embedded objects.

12. (i) Place the cursor in the location where you want the symbol to appear.

(ii) On the Insert menu select Special Character.

(iii) In the dialog that appears, choose Symbol from the Font list. The copyright symbol is available in a Serif font (character 212) or in a San-Serif font (character 228). ...

(iv) Click OK.

13. When working with large spreadsheets containing a considerable number of rows or columns with data, it is often needed autosum with a quick click of a menu or button instead of manually typing the SUM function. OpenOffice spreadsheet program Calc has this feature.

(i) Open any Calc workbook with numbers and data, or open your workbook.

(ii) Select the cell where you would like to put the autosum of your data.

(iii) Click on the sigma icon beside the formula bar and click Sum from the dropdown menu. You can see the Sum is calculated automatically.

14. AdmissionNo should be set as the primary key because admission numbers are unique for each and every student of the school, which is not possible in the case of RollNo and Name.

15. Two advantages of networking are as follows :

(i) **User Communication** Network allows users to communicate using emails, social networking sites, video conferencing, etc.

(ii) **File Sharing** By using networking data or information can be shared or transferred from one computer to another.

16. The main purpose of a blog is to convey messages about events, announcements, need, review etc. Blogs are usually managed using a web browser and this requires active internet connection.

17. A Scenario is a set of values that Calc saves for a group of cells. Whenever we run a scenario Calc automatically substitutes the saved cell values into a connected formula to give us an output. By having different scenarios for a same group of cells we can get different results from the formula and compare these results to know which is the most suitable set of values for us. For example, if you wanted to calculate the effect of different interest rates on a car loan, you could add a scenario for each interest rate, and quickly view the results. This will help you to easily find out the most desirable rate of interest for availing the loan. Clearly a Scenario is a tool to test "what-if" questions (What happens if I replace THIS value by THAT value ••.). Each scenario has a name, and can be edited and formatted separately. You can easily switch between different scenarios for a group of cells by using the scenario drop down list or scenario navigator.

18. Writer does not update the table of contents automatically, so after any changes to the headings, you must update it manually.

1. To update a table of contents when changes are made to the document:
   (i) Right-click anywhere in the TOC.
   (ii) From the pop-up menu, choose Update Index/Table. Writer updates the table of contents to reflect the changes in the document.

   You can also update the index from the Navigator by right-clicking on Indexes > Table of Contents1 and choosing Index > Update from the pop-up menu.

2. To delete the table of contents from a document:
   (i) Right-click anywhere in the TOC.
   (ii) From the pop-up menu, choose Delete Index/Table. Writer deletes the table of contents.

19. (i) There are 6 fields and 7 records in the table SummerCamp.

(ii) (a) SELECT * FROM SummerCamp WHERE DOB BETWEEN 02/02/09 AND 06/03/10;

    (b) SELECT * FROM SummerCamp WHERE Gender='F';

    (c) SELECT * FROM SummerCamp ORDER BY First Name;

20. (a) Database Management System (DBMS) is a collection of programs that enable users to create, maintain database and control all the access to the database. The primary goal of the DBMS is to provide an environment that is both convenient and efficient for user to retrieve and store information.

(b) The advantages of using DBMS for school are as follows:
   (i) In school, DBMS is used to store the data about students, teachers and any other related things at a centralised location.
   (ii) It provides security to the personal information of the school, stored in it.

21. Differences between star topology and bus topology are as follows:

	Star topology	Bus topology
(i)	All the nodes are directly connected with the central node or server.	There is a single length of transmission medium, on which various nodes are attached and the server can be anywhere in the transmission cable.
(ii)	Faults can be easily detected.	Faults cannot be easily detected.
(iii)	It has fast transmission speed.	It becomes slow as the number of nodes increases.

SAMPLE
QUESTION
PAPER 7

Information Technology

Time : **2 hrs**   Max. Marks : **50**

Instructions

1. Please read the instructions carefully
2. This Question Paper consists of 21 questions in two sections: Section A & Section B.
3. Section A has Objective type questions whereas Section B contains Subjective type questions.
4. Out of the given (5 + 16 =) 21 questions, a candidate has to answer (5 + 10 =) 15 questions in the allotted (maximum) time of 2 hours.
5. All questions of a particular section must be attempted in the correct order.
6. Section A : Objective Type Questions (24 Marks)
   (i) This section has 05 questions.
   (ii) Marks allotted are mentioned against each question/part.
   (iii) There is no negative marking.
   (iv) Do as per the instructions given.
7. Section B: Subjective Type Questions (26 Marks)
   (i) This section has 16 questions.
   (ii) A candidate has to do 10 questions.
   (iii) Do as per the instructions given.
   (iv) Marks allotted are mentioned against each question/part.

Section-A

(Objective Type Questions)

1. Answer any 4 out of the given 6 questions based on Employability Skills   [1 × 4 = 4 Marks]

   (i) .... is the means by which a message is sent between devices.   [1]
       (a) Data   (b) Channel
       (c) Receiver   (d) None of these

(ii) .... stress is a result of body's response to deal with a dangerous situation or escape from it. [1]

    (a) Internal   (b) Environmental

    (c) External   (d) Survival

(iii) An operating system that manages a group of independent computers and makes them appear to be a single computer is known as a .... operating system. [1]

    (a) real-time   (b) Graphical

    (c) distributed   (d) Multi-user

(iv) An entrepreneur must form contacts with the .... to analyse the market. [1]

    (a) Planning   (b) Competitors

    (c) neighbours   (d) None of these

(v) .... brings about changes in people's knowledge, attitude and skills. [1]

    (a) Sustainable development   (b) Natural resources

    (c) Both (a) and (b)   (d) None of these

(vi) .... plays a major role in reaction to stress. [1]

    (a) Personality   (b) Positive attitude

    (c) Behaviour   (d) None of these

2. Answer any 5 out of the given 6 questions   [1 × 5 = 5 Marks]

(i) Which client software is used to request and display web pages? [1]

    (a) Web server   (b) FTP

    (c) Multimedia   (d) Web browser

(ii) The default data type for a field is .... [1]

    (a) char   (b) int   (c) text   (d) None of these

(iii) Alpana has made four spreadsheets containing marks of 5 subjects of all the students of her class. She has to prepare a sheet that contains the total marks of all the students of her class. Name the option that can be used to perform this task. [1]

    (a) Subtotal   (b) Average   (c) Goal Seek   (d) Scenario

(iv) Field is the individual sub component of one .... [1]

    (a) record   (b) column

    (c) data   (d) None of these

(v) In the Mail Merge dialog box, you can select the .... option if you want to save the merged documents. [1]

    (a) File   (b) Edit   (c) View   (d) Format

(vi) You create a table in MS-Access. You decided to create two fields RollNo and Date of Birth, what will be the data type of Date-of-Birth column? [1]

    (a) Number   (b) Yes/No   (c) Text   (d) Date/Time

3. Answer any 5 out of the given 6 questions   [1 × 5 = 5 Marks]

(i) Prerna is a student of class X. Her teacher has asked her to create a document on 'Women Empowerment'. She has written the text and also added relevant images in her document using Writer. But she has realised that the paragraph will look better if the images are placed around the text. Name the feature of writer she can use to get the desired result. [1]

    (a) Placing image   (b) Positioning image

    (c) Wrap text   (d) Closing text

(ii) Linked data is stored in the .... [1]

    (a) destination file   (b) web file

    (c) source file   (d) domain file

(iii) Internet is a network of ....   [1]
    (a) networks   (b) data
    (c) value   (d) pages

(iv) The grey colour in the TOC reminds us that the text has been generated ....   [1]
    (a) manually   (b) automatically
    (c) Both (a) and (b)   (d) None of these

(v) .... is used in between the cell reference in a formula.   [1]
    (a):   (b),
    (c) Both (a) and (b)   (d) @

(vi) Internally for each recorded macro, some code is generated, which is stored inside .... and .... clause.   [1]
    (a) Sub, End Sub   (b) Section, End Section
    (c) Function, End Function   (d) None of these

4. Answer any 5 out of the given 6 questions   [1 × 5 = 5 Marks]

  (i) The first network ever developed was ....   [1]
    (a) ARPANET   (b) Internet   (c) NSFnet   (d) NET

 (ii) Prashant is a writer. He has just completed writing his book using Writer software. Now, he wants to add a page which will contain the title of each chapter and its respective page number. Suggest the feature that can be used to do this task.   [1]
    (a) Mail merge   (b) Templates
    (c) Styles   (d) Table of contents

(iii) .... is the blank space between the worksheet data and the edges of the printed page.   [1]
    (a) Field space   (b) Data space
    (c) Margins   (d) Description box

(iv) A/An .... that identifies a specific computer on the Internet.   [1]
    (a) user name   (b) domain name   (c) E-mail   (d) None of these

 (v) Satellites which are orbiting around the .... , provide necessary links for telephone and television service.   [1]
    (a) space   (b) Earth   (c) station   (d) All of these

(vi) Template includes .... text that is surrounded by brackets.   [1]
    (a) margin   (b) placeholder   (c) data source   (d) track changes

5. Answer any 5 out of the given 6 questions   [1 × 5 = 5 Marks]

  (i) Duplication of data is known as ....   [1]
    (a) data security   (b) data incomplete
    (c) data redundancy   (d) None of these

 (ii) The term .... is derived from the words interconnection and networks.   [1]
    (a) connection   (b) Internet
    (c) Both (a) and (b)   (d) None of these

(iii) To create a hyperlink to a webpage, FTP server of Telnet connection, click on the .... icon.   [1]
    (a) internet explorer   (b) Internet
    (c) hyperlink   (d) document

(iv) In www, a client is called ....   [1]
    (a) web server   (b) web page

      (c) web browser   (d) None of these

(v) Priya, Ravi and Suresh are working in the accounts department of an advertising company. They handle different set of clients. Now they are collaborating to create a spreadsheet for maintaining records of all their clients combined together. Which option should they use so that they all can work simultaneously in the sheet?   **[1]**

    (a) Add document   (b) Share document

    (c) Combine document   (d) None of these

(vi) A router passes data packets from one network to another network based on their .... not MAC address.   **[1]**

    (a) IP address   (b) URL

    (c) Web address   (d) None of these

Section-B

(Subjective Type Questions)

- Answer any 3 out of the given 5 questions on Employability skills.   [2 × 3 = 6 Marks]
- Answer each question in 20-30 words.

6. What do you mean by verbal communication?   [2]

7. Explain the term fatigue related stress.   [2]

8. What are the responsibilities of an operating system with respect to file management?   [2]

9. What are the disadvantages of entrepreneurship?   [2]

10. Describe any two problems related to sustainable development.   [2]

- Answer any 4 out of the given 6 questions in 20-30 words each.   [2 × 4 = 8 Marks]

11. What is Mail Merge?   [2]

12. What is a macro?   [2]

13. What is the role of key fields in a database? Name the keys in a DBMS.   [2]

14. How does a router help in maintaining a network ?   [2]

15. Define the following terms: [2]

    (i) Active Cell   (ii) Sheet Tab

16. How can a document's style be changed ? Explain with proper steps.   [2]

- Answer any 3 out of the given 5 questions in 50-80 words each.   [4 × 3 = 12 Marks]

17. Ishita is a teacher. She had entered the marks of all the students and also calculated the total of the students. Now, she wants to sort the data so that she can find the names of the students according to their marks in descending order. Tell her the different steps to sort the data.   [4]

18. Write the steps for text fitting inside a shape in a word processor document. Also, describe its options.   [4]

19. Consider the following table : Employee Salary.   [4]

Table : EmployeeSalary

LastName	FirstName	Dept	PayrollNumber	Salary (₹)	JobTitle
Shen	James	Finance	A621	19500	Payroll Clerk
Gupta	Shruthi	Finance	M502	35000	Accountant
Bedi	Reeta	Human Resource	M421	18500	Secretary
Walker	Tia	Sales	W815	24000	Sales Represen-tative
Shafia	Ahmed	Factory	H219	39000	Factory Manager
Mittal	Chavi	Purchasing	M134	20000	Purchasing Clerk

(i) How many fields and records are there in the table Employee Salary

(ii) Write the SQL queries for the following:

    (a) List all data of table EmployeeSalary.

    (b) Display all the records whose salary is less than 25000.

    (c) Display the FirstName and JobTitle of employees having Dept 'Finance'.

20. What do you mean by data control language? Also, give its types.   [4]

21. How to clear web history on the Mozilla Firefox browser?   [4]

Answers

1. (i)(b), (ii)(d),(iii)(c),(iv)(b),(v)(a),(vi)(a)

2. (i)(d), (ii)(c),(iii)(a),(iv)(a),(v)(a),(vi)(d)

3. (i)(c), (ii)(c),(iii)(a),(iv)(b),(v)(c),(vi)(a)

4. (i)(a), (ii)(d),(iii)(c),(iv)(b),(v)(b),(vi)(b)

5. (i)(c), (ii)(b),(iii)(b),(iv)(c),(v)(b),(vi)(a)

6. Verbal communication means communication through spoken oral and written words. It implies use of words which make up a language. It is the ability to communicate using words in understandable language i.e. English, Hindi, French, Urdu etc. Language play a significant role in verbal communication. The effectiveness of the verbal communication depends on the tone of the speaker, clarity of speech, volume, speed, body language and the quality of words used in conversation.

7. Fatigue related kind of stress builds up over a long time like by working too long or too hard at our job, school or home. It can also be caused by exercising too much or too long. If you do not know how to manage your time well or how to take time out for rest and relaxation, you will become a victim of fatigue related stress. This can be one of the hardest kinds of stresses to avoid because many people feel that it is out of their control.

8. The operating system is responsible for the following activities in connection with file management :

- Allocating and deallocating memory space as needed.
- Creating and deleting files.
- Creating and deleting directories to organise files.
- Supporting primitives for manipulating files and directories.
- Mapping files onto secondary storage.
- Backing up files on stable (non-volatile) storage media.

9. Some of the disadvantages of entrepreneurship are as follows :

- **Huge Amount of Time** You have to dedicate a huge amount of time to your own business. Entrepreneurship is not easy and for it to be successful, you have to take a level of time commitment.
- **Risk** An entrepreneurship involves high risk of loss. If the business fails then it will wipe away all the personal savings.
- **Hard Work** An entrepreneur has to work very hard to make the new business very successful.
- **Uncertain Income** There is no regular or fixed income available to an entrepreneur. So, there is uncertain kind of income received by an entrepreneur.

10. Two problems related to sustainable development are as follows:

- Poor management of natural resources combined with growing economic activities will continue to pose serious challenges to environment.
- The most significant environmental problems are associated with resources that are renewable such as air and water. They have finite capacity to assimilate emissions and wastes but if pollution exceeds this capacity, ecosystem can deteriorate rapidly.

11. Mail Merge is a very important feature of word processor. It is used to create a series of documents with same text and multiple addresses. In the process of mail merge we merge a main document (a letter or certificate etc.) with different mailing addresses to create several copies of the main document bearing addresses of different individuals. Mail merge is generally used to send invitations, letters or to print certificates for several people.

12. A macro is a saved sequence of commands or keystrokes that are stored for later use. An example of a simple macro is one that "types" your address. The Libre Office macro language is very flexible, allowing automation of both simple and complex tasks. Macros are especially useful to repeat a task the same way over and over again.

13. The key is defined as the column or the set of columns of the database table which is used to identify each record uniquely in a relation. If a table has id, name and address as the column names then each one is known as the *key* for that table. The key field is a unique identifier for each record.

Alternate, foreign, primary and candidate are a few types of keys in a DBMS.

14. A hardware device designed to take incoming packets, analyse the packets, move the packets to another network. convert the packets to another network interface, drop the packets, direct packets to the appropriate locations, etc. A router functions similar to a bridge. However, unlike a bridge, a router passes data packets from one network to another network based on their IP addresses not MAC addresses.

15. (i) **Active Cell** The cell with the black outline in a spreadsheet Data is always entered into the active cell.

  (ii) **Sheet Tab** The tab at the bottom of a worksheet tells you the name of the worksheet such as Sheet 1, Sheet 2 etc. Switching between worksheets can be done by clicking on the tab of the Sheet which you want to access.

16. **Changing a style using the Style dialog box** To change an existing style using the Style dialog, right-click on the required style in the Styles and Formatting window and select **Modify** from the pop-up menu.

The Style dialog displayed depends on the type of style selected. Each style dialog has several tabs. See the chapters on styles in the user guides for details.

To update a style from a selection:

Step 1 Open the Styles and Formatting dialog.

Step 2 In the document, select an item that has the format you want to adopt as a style.

Step 3 In the Styles and Formatting dialog, select the style you want to update (single-click, not double-click), then long-click on the arrow next to the New Style from Selection icon and click on Update Style.

AutoUpdate applies to paragraph and frame styles only. If the AutoUpdate option is selected on the Organizer page of the Paragraph Style or Frame Style dialog, applying direct formatting to a paragraph or frame using this style in your document automatically updates the style itself. You can also update styles by copying or loading them from a template or another document

17. Ishita can Highlight the cells to be sorted, then select Data > Sort to open the Sort dialog, or click the Sort Ascending or Sort Descending toolbar buttons. Using the dialog, you can sort the selected cells using up to three columns, in either ascending (A-Z, 1-9) or descending (Z-A, 9-1) order.

18. Assume you want to create some shapes which have text in them. Some of the text might wrap within the shape.To do this,you have to right-click and choose Text and go back to the Texty Tab and check the option Word wrap Text in Shape. In this way,the text gets wrapped inside a shape.You can also resize the shape to fit text.

To format the text in a shape Select the object to which text was added. Select Format > Text or right-click on the shape and select Text from the pop-up menu. The Text dialog is displayed.

19. (i) There are 6 fields and 6 records in the table EmployeeSalary.

(ii) (a) SELECT * FROM EmployeeSalary;

(b) SELECT * FROM EmployeeSalary WHERE Salary<25000;

(c) SELECT FirstName, JobTitle FROM EmployeeSalary WHERE Dept='Finance';

20. DCL (Data Control Language) commands are used to assign security levels in database which involves multiple user setups. They are used to grant defined roles and access privileges to the users.

There are two kinds of user in the schema

Step 1 Users They work with the data, but cannot change the structure of the schema. They write data manipulation language.

Step 2 Admin They can change the structure of the schema and control access to the schema objects. They write data definition language.

Step 3 Basically, the DCL component of the SQL language is used to create privileges that allow to users access and manipulation of the database.

Two types of DCL commands are :

(i) GRANT Used to give user's access privileges to database.

(ii) REVOKE Used to withdraw access privileges given with the GRANT command.

21. Follow the steps below to clear the web history on the Mozilla Firefox browser:

Step 1 Click on the upper right of the browser toolbar.

Step 2 Click History.

Step 3 Click Clear Recent History.

Step 4 Click the drop-down menu next to Time range to clear and select everything.

Step 5 Place a checkmark next to the following options under Details:

Step 6 Browsing and Download History • Form and Search History • Cookies

Step 7 Cache • Active Logins • Offline Website Data

Step 8 Site Preferences

Step 9 Click on clear Now button.

SAMPLE QUESTION PAPER 8

Information Technology

Time : **2 hrs**　Max. Marks : **50**

Instructions

1. Please read the instructions carefully
2. This Question Paper consists of 21 questions in two sections: Section A & Section B.
3. Section A has Objective type questions whereas Section B contains Subjective type questions.
4. Out of the given (5 + 16 =) 21 questions, a candidate has to answer (5 + 10 =) 15 questions in the allotted (maximum) time of 2 hours.
5. All questions of a particular section must be attempted in the correct order.
6. Section A : Objective Type Questions (24 Marks)
   (i) This section has 05 questions.
   (ii) Marks allotted are mentioned against each question/part.
   (iii) There is no negative marking.
   (iv) Do as per the instructions given.
7. Section B: Subjective Type Questions (26 Marks)
   (i) This section has 16 questions.
   (ii) A candidate has to do 10 questions.
   (iii) Do as per the instructions given.
   (iv) Marks allotted are mentioned against each question/part.

Section-A

(Objective Type Questions)

1. Answer any 4 out of the given 6 questions based on Employability Skills　　[1 × 4 = 4 Marks]

　(i) ……… barriers are created in the mind by none other than ourselves, through preconceived notions and the stereotyping of people.　　[1]

　　(a) Imaginative　　　　　　(b) Perceptual

　　(c) Language　　　　　　　(d) Cultural

(ii) Regular exercise helps pep up your mood and can take your mind off a lot of worry and negativity which are the main feed of stress. Which of the following activity is not considered as exercise? [1]

   (a) Walking   (b) Jogging   (c) Swimming   (d) Talking

(iii) Moving a folder or a file means .... it from its original location and placing it at another location. [1]

   (a) Removing   (b) Leaving

   (c) Pointing   (d) None of these

(iv) Which of the following sentences is in passive voice? [1]

   (a) By whom was the mess cleaned?   (b) The birds were being fed by my sister.

   (c) Uncle Rakesh teaches my brother.   (d) Both (a) and (b)

(v) Kaspersky, McAfee are examples of popular .... [1]

   (a) image editing software   (b) anti-virus software

   (c) word-processing software   (d) DBMS

(vi) .... builds up over a period of time and takes a toll on the body due to overwork. [1]

   (a) Fatigue   (c) Irritability

   (b) Depression   (d) None of these

2. Answer any 5 out of the given 6 questions   [1 × 5 = 5 Marks]

  (i) A person who writes a blog or a weblog is known as .... [1]

   (a) program   (b) user

   (c) blogger   (d) None of these

(ii) The .... command is used to modify the existing rows in a table. [1]

   (a) UPDATE   (b) SELECT   (c) INSERT   (d) REVIEW

(iii) A...............is a database element that is used to view, enter and edit records in a table. [1]

   (a) Form   (b) Report

   (c) Query   (d) None of these

(iv) Neeta is planning to take a car loan to buy a new car. But she is not sure about the payback time, i.e. whether to pay it back in 5 or 6 years considering that her monthly fuel cost will also increase. In such cases, which of the following features of spreadsheet can she use to get an idea about it? [1]

   (a) Consolidation   (b) Macros

   (c) Templates   (d) What-if analysis

(v) .... styles are used to format graphics and text frames, including text wrap, borders, backgrounds and columns. [1]

   (a) Border   (b) Frame   (c) Table   (d) Text

(vi) A .... language is a portion of a DML involving information retrieval only. [1]

   (a) DCL   (b) Query

   (c) TCL   (d) None of these

3. Answer any 5 out of the given 6 questions   [1 × 5 = 5 Marks]

  (i) This is a type of hyperlink available in Hyperlink dialog box, which creates a new worksheet. [1]

   (a) New document   (b) New file

   (c) New worksheet   (d) New data

(ii) The processed form of data is known as .... [1]

   (a) value   (b) information

   (c) knowledge   (d) None of these

(iii) .... service can integrate both video calling and instant messaging abilities. [1]

    (a) Web conferencing   (b) Web browser

    (c) Web page   (d) None of these

(iv) ....is a list, usually found on a page before the start of a written work, of its chapter or section titles or brief descriptions with their commencing page numbers. [1]

    (a) Preface   (b) Table of contents

    (c) Acknowledgements   (d) Page title

(v) For sorting through macro, the selected cell range must be .... [1]

    (a) identical   (b) different

    (c) Both (a) and (b)   (d) formatted

(vi) To add a new image to the Gallery, you can click on the .... button. [1]

    (a) New image   (b) Add image

    (c) New theme   (d) Add theme

4. Answer any 5 out of the given 6 questions   [1 × 5 = 5 Marks]

(i) A collection of web pages linked together in a random order is .... [1]

    (a) a website   (b) a web server

    (c) a search engine   (d) a web browser

(ii) .... are descriptions about the changes made in cells during record changes mode. [1]

    (a) Tips   (b) Comments

    (c) Messages   (d) None of these

(iii) State whether True or False.

    Duplicate values can be entered in column marked as primary key. [1]

    (a) True   (b) False

(iv) .... are used for transmitting data across networks. [1]

    (a) Circuit switching   (b) Switching techniques

    (c) Channel   (d) None of these

(v) The speed of a network is measured in .... [1]

    (a) mbps   (b) bytes

    (c) kHz   (d) None of these

(vi) Which of the following is not a required information for Label set-up? [1]

    (a) Height   (b) Number

    (c) Vertical pitch   (d) Column

5. Answer any 5 out of the given 6 questions   [1 × 5 = 5 Marks]

(i) What data type should be chosen for a zipcode field in a table? [1]

    (a) Tat   (b) Number

    (c) Memo   (d) All of these

(ii) Wireless broadband can be .... [1]

    (a) mobile   (b) fixed

    (c) Both (a) and (b)   (d) None of these

(iii) The candidate key, which is not used as primary key is called .... key. [1]

    (a) primary   (b) foreign

    (c) alternate   (d) super

(iv) A table in a relational database is also called as............... [1]

    (a) tuple   (b) records

    (c) results   (d) relation

(v) A ....can also be a quick way to take a list of people's mailing addresses and generate labels or envelopes with the address for a different person on each label or envelope.   [1]

(a) data source   (b) database

(c) mail merge   (d) E-mail

(vi) .... is the formation of networks.   [1]

(a) Server   (b) Networking

(c) Client   (d) None of these

Section-B

(Subjective Type Questions)

- Answer any 3 out of the given 5 questions on Employability skills.   [2 × 3 = 6 Marks]
- Answer each question in 20-30 words.

6. What do you mean by non-verbal communication?   [2]

7. Explain the term self-motivation.   [2]

8. Define multi-processing and multi-user operating system.   [2]

9. What do you mean by the term entrepreneur?   [2]

10. What is the importance and need of sustainable development?   [2]

- Answer any 4 out of the given 6 questions in 20-30 words each.   [2 × 4 = 8 Marks]

11. Describe the significance of using templates in your documents.   [2]

12. State the use of Consolidating Data in a spreadsheet.   [2]

13. Explain the Text and Memo data types.   [2]

14. Explain the term table used in database.   [2]

15. Distinguish between repeater and switch.   [2]

16. What are the steps to apply first aid roller bandage to a wound?   [2]

- Answer any 3 out of the given 5 questions in 50-80 words each.   [4 × 3 = 12 Marks]

17. Harmanpreet had inserted an image in a word processor application. Now, she wants to know the use of the following terms. Tell her the correct answer.   [4]

(i) Alignment   (ii) Anchoring   (iii) Rotating   (iv) Resizing

18. Samiksha wants to know the use of the following terms. Describe them for her.   [4]

(i) Goal Seek   (ii) Scenario   (iii) Subtotal   (iv) Solver

19. Consider the following table APPLICANTS   [4]

TABLE: APPLICANTS

No.	NAME	FEE	GENDER	C_ID	JOINYEAR
1012	Amandeep	30000	M	A01	2012
1102	Avisha	25000	F	A02	2009
1103	Ekant	30000	M	A02	2011
1049	Arun	30000	M	A03	2009
1025	Amber	40000	M	A02	2011

(i) How many records and fields are there in the table APPLICANTS.

(ii) Write the SQL queries to:

   (a) Display NAME, FEE, GENDER, JOINYEAR about the APPLICANTS, who have joined before 2010.

   (b) Display the NAMES of all APPLICANTS in ascending order of their JOINYEAR.

   (c) Display the NAMES of all APPLICANTS in ascending order of their JOINYEAR.

20. Prashant wants to know about Data Manipulation language commands. Solve the following queries for him.   [4]

(i) What is DML?   (ii) Write the use of any three DML commands.

21. Chetanya wants to know the functions of the following terms. Tell him the correct answer.   [4]

(i) Modem   (ii) Web page   (iii) Wi-fi   (iv) GPS

Answers

1. (i)(b), (ii)(d),(iii)(a),(iv)(d),(v)(b),(vi)(a)

2. (i)(c), (ii)(a),(iii)(a),(iv)(d),(v)(b),(vi)(c)

3. (i)(a), (ii)(a),(iii)(a),(iv)(d),(v)(c),(vi)(c)

4. (i)(a), (ii)(b),(iii)(b),(iv)(c),(v)(a),(vi)(b)

5. (i)(b), (ii)(c),(iii)(c),(iv)(d),(v)(a),(vi)(b)

SAMPLE
QUESTION
PAPER 9

Information Technology

Time : **2 hrs**   Max. Marks : **50**

Instructions

1. Please read the instructions carefully
2. This Question Paper consists of 21 questions in two sections: Section A & Section B.
3. Section A has Objective type questions whereas Section B contains Subjective type questions.
4. Out of the given (5 + 16 =) 21 questions, a candidate has to answer (5 + 10 =) 15 questions in the allotted (maximum) time of 2 hours.
5. All questions of a particular section must be attempted in the correct order.
6. Section A : Objective Type Questions (24 Marks)
    (i) This section has 05 questions.
    (ii) Marks allotted are mentioned against each question/part.
    (iii) There is no negative marking.
    (iv) Do as per the instructions given.
7. Section B: Subjective Type Questions (26 Marks)
    (i) This section has 16 questions.
    (ii) A candidate has to do 10 questions.
    (iii) Do as per the instructions given.
    (iv) Marks allotted are mentioned against each question/part.

Section-A

(Objective Type Questions)

1. Answer any 4 out of the given 6 questions based on Employability Skills   [1 × 4 = 4 Marks]

    (i) .... is the first screen that is displayed after switching on the Windows.   [1]

        (a) My computer   (b) Desktop

        (c) Windows   (d) Login

(ii) Coherent is one of the 7 C's of effecting communication. It means, the communication should be smooth and .... [1]

   (a) logical   (b) long   (c) short   (d) specific

(iii) Stress management infuses a sense of .... and accomplishment. [1]

   (a) pressure   (b) control

   (c) threat   (d) None of these

(iv) A .... is a network security device that monitors incoming and outgoing network. It restricts access to unwanted sites. [1]

   (a) firewall   (b) anti-virus

   (c) block sites   (d) None of these

(v) .... are the people who are too focused on what others think and they fail to focus on their internal matters. [1]

   (a) Seekers   (b) Introspectors

   (c) Gold diggers   (d) Pleasers

(vi) Please pass me the sauce. This sentence is a type of............sentence. [1]

   (a) assertive   (b) interrogative

   (c) imperative   (d) exclamatory

2. Answer any 5 out of the given 6 questions   [1 × 5 = 5 Marks]

  (i) abc@mnc.co.in represents an .... [1]

   (a) MAC address   (b) URL

   (c) E-mail address   (d) None of these

(ii) Which of the following fields will not make a suitable primary key? [1]

   (a) A customer's account number   (b) A date-field

   (c) An auto number field   (d) A student's admission number

(iii) A............allows you to present data retrieved from one or more tables so that, it can be analysed and printed, if required. [1]

   (a) report   (b) form   (c) table   (d) query

(iv) Goal Seek is also called as............is one of the What-if analysis tools that is available in Calc. [1]

   (a) back-solving   (b) solver

   (c) forward-solving   (d) result analysis

(v) If you choose styles, and then change the base style then all the .... styles will change as well. [1]

   (a) linked   (b) edited

   (c) copied   (d) None of these

(vi) Which one of the following is an example of RDBMS ? [1]

   (a) MongoDB   (b) Windows registry

   (c) Publisher   (d) Oracle

3. Answer any 5 out of the given 6 questions   [1 × 5 = 5 Marks]

  (i) Which tab of writer contains the Hyperlink option? [1]

   (a) File   (b) Format

   (c) Insert   (d) Tools

(ii) To insert a symbol like © (copyright), you need to click on the............option of the Insert tab. [1]

   (a) Special Character   (b) Character

   (c) Equation   (d) Header

(iii) Digital information is converted into analog information by the modem at [1]
    (a) destination computer   (b) source computer
    (c) Both (a) and (b)   (d) Neither (a) nor (b)

(iv) To delete a template, ... on a template in the Templates window and select delete. [1]
    (a) Right-click   (b) Left-click
    (c) Double-click   (d) None of these

(v) If you see #### in place of data in a cell, it means you need to .... the cell width. [1]
    (a) increase   (b) decrease
    (c) Both (a) and (b)   (d) None of these

(vi) When a user inserts a new worksheet in spreadsheet software, the new worksheet will be inserted .... [1]
    (a) at the end of sheet tab   (b) in the beginning of sheet tab
    (c) next to active sheet   (d) None of these

4. Answer any 5 out of the given 6 questions   [1 × 5 = 5 Marks]

(i) A group of computers connected together with the help of cables within an office building is called [1]
    (a) PAN   (b) MAN
    (c) WAN   (d) LAN

(ii) Which of the following is not a style type in Writer? [1]
    (a) Frame style   (b) Image style
    (c) List style   (d) Character style

(iii) A primary key field cannot be null, which also means that it cannot be .... [1]
    (a) invalid   (b) positive
    (c) alphanumeric   (d) empty

(iv) Which of the following websites is used for booking train tickets? [1]
    (a) Nykaa   (b) IRCTC
    (c) RedBus   (d) Myntra

(v) Which of the following is an application based instant messaging software? [1]
    (a) Google Talk   (b) eBuddy
    (c) Meebo   (d) MSN Web Messenger

(vi) In the given formula, identify the type of reference and the cells that are passed as arguments.
= Average(A5, B5) [1]
    (a) Absolute reference; cells are-A5 and B5
    (b) Relative reference; cells are-A5 and B5
    (c) Relative reference; cells are-A5 to B5
    (d) Absolute reference; cells are-A5 to B5

5. Answer any 5 out of the given 6 questions   [1 × 5 = 5 Marks]

(i) Information is the processed form of .... [1]
    (a) words   (b) data   (c) sentence   (d) records

(ii) .... is the act of posting content on a blog. [1]
    (a) Edublog   (b) Posting
    (c) Blogging   (d) Blogger

(iii) DBMS provides various key fields as [1]
    (a) primary key and candidate key   (b) alternate key and foreign key
    (c) Both (a) and (b)   (d) None of these

(iv) In order to use data from a worksheet, you need to use its............ name. [1]
    (a) alias   (b) representative
    (c) qualified   (d) quantified

(v) You can move a dockable window to a convenient position on the screen by holding down the ....key and drag it by the title bar to where you want it docked. [1]
    (a) Ctrl   (b) Alt
    (c) Shift   (d) Windows

(vi) Instant messaging service accepts instant messages from [1]
    (a) external sites   (b) internal sites
    (c) Both (a) and (b)   (d) None of these

Section-B

(Subjective Type Questions)

- Answer any 3 out of the given 5 questions on Employability skills.   [2 × 3 = 6 Marks]
- Answer each question in 20-30 words.

6. Explain the parts of speech. [2]

7. What do you mean by survival stress? [2]

8. Explain the use of Antivirus for the protection of the computer system. [2]

9. Describe the role of entrepreneurs. [2]

10. What are the uses of sustainable development? [2]

- Answer any 4 out of the given 6 questions in 20-30 words each.   [2 × 4 = 8 Marks]

11. Mention the steps to be followed choose a style for a Word document? [2]

12. Write the steps to freeze the columns. [2]

13. What do you mean by relative cell referencing? [2]

14. Describe various transaction control commands of SQL. [2]

15. Explain the working of message switching technique. [2]

16. Define the following : [2]
    (i) Accident in workplace   (ii) Hazard

- Answer any 3 out of the given 5 questions in 50-80 words each.   [4 × 3 = 12 Marks]

17. Tanisha had created a Table of Contents of the project done by her. Tell her the different steps to do the following: [4]
    (a) Editing a TOC   (b) Updating a TOC

18. Simran wants to add comments in a spreadsheet application. Tell her the different steps involved of adding and editing comments. [4]

19. Consider the following table ITEMS :   [4]

TABLE: ITEMS

Code	IName	Qty	Price	Company	TCode
1001	DIGITAL PAD 121	120	11000	XENITA	T01
1006	LED SCREEN 40	70	38000	SANTORA	T02
1004	CAR GPS SYSTEM	50	2150	GEOKNOW	T01
1003	DIGITAL CAMERA 12X	160	8000	DIGICLICK	T02
1005	PEN DRIVE 32 GB	600	1200	STOREHOME	T03

(a) How many fields and records are there in the table ITEMS?

(b) Write the SQL queries to:

   (i) Display the detail of all the items in ascending order of item names (i.e., IName)

   (ii) Display IName and Price of all those items, whose price is in the range of 10000 and 22000.

   (iii) Display all the information of the items having price less than 10000.

20. Nupur wants to know the differences between the following: [4]

(a) Fields and tuples

(b) Data and information

21. Lakshit wants to know the definitions of the following terms. Answer to his query :   [4]

   (i) Web based instant messaging software

   (ii) Cable modem.

Answers

1. (i)(b), (ii)(c), (iii)(a), (iv)(a), (v)(b), (vi)(c)

2. (i)(c), (ii)(b), (iii)(a), (iv)(a), (v)(a), (vi)(d)

3. (i)(c), (ii)(a), (iii)(b), (iv)(a), (v)(b), (vi)(a)

4. (i)(d), (ii)(b), (iii)(d), (iv)(b), (v)(a), (vi)(a)

5. (i)(d), (ii)(c), (iii)(c), (iv)(a), (v)(a), (vi)(c)

SAMPLE QUESTION PAPER 10

Information Technology

Time : **2 hrs**   Max. Marks : **50**

Instructions

1. Please read the instructions carefully
2. This Question Paper consists of 21 questions in two sections: Section A & Section B.
3. Section A has Objective type questions whereas Section B contains Subjective type questions.
4. Out of the given (5 + 16 =) 21 questions, a candidate has to answer (5 + 10 =) 15 questions in the allotted (maximum) time of 2 hours.
5. All questions of a particular section must be attempted in the correct order.
6. Section A : Objective Type Questions (24 Marks)
    (i) This section has 05 questions.
    (ii) Marks allotted are mentioned against each question/part.
    (iii) There is no negative marking.
    (iv) Do as per the instructions given.
7. Section B: Subjective Type Questions (26 Marks)
    (i) This section has 16 questions.
    (ii) A candidate has to do 10 questions.
    (iii) Do as per the instructions given.
    (iv) Marks allotted are mentioned against each question/part.

Section-A

(Objective Type Questions)

1. Answer any 4 out of the given 6 questions based on Employability Skills   [1 × 4 = 4 Marks]

(i) …………… is an effective method to learn the art of freely interacting with people, at the same time boosting your self-confidence.   [1]

    (a) Listening   (b) Public speaking

    (c) Playing   (d) Working out

(ii) Which of the following is not a symptom of stress? [1]
 (a) Irritability   (b) Insomnia
 (c) Fatigue   (d) Fever

(iii) When you start a computer, the operating system gets loaded into the main memory from the hard disk. This is called .... [1]
 (a) uploading   (b) booting
 (c) starting   (d) downloading

(iv) Unless the students are clear about their learning target, ... is irrelevant. [1]
 (a) feedback   (b) solution
 (c) Both (a) and (b)   (d) None of these

(v) .... is a windows utility that consolidates fragmented files and folders on your computer's hard disk. [1]
 (a) Disk cleanup   (b) Disk consolidation
 (c) Disk defragmenter   (d) None of these

(vi) The drive within you that compels you to complete tasks is [1]
 (a) self-motivation   (b) self-regulation
 (c) self-awareness   (d) self-sufficient

2. Answer any 5 out of the given 6 questions [1 × 5 = 5 Marks]

(i) Do not use the elevator in times of fire in the building. Always use .... for such emergencies. [1]
 (a) office space (b) staircase (c) washroom (d) None of these

(ii) Databases have the ability to [1]
 (a) store a large amount of data in a structured format, easy update, sort query, production of reports.
 (b) spell check, perform calculations, library of mathematical functions, replication.
 (c) rotate images, copy and paste, fill scale.
 (d) None of the above

(iii) Solve option under Tools menu amounts to a more elaborate form of .... The difference is that the Solver deals with equations with multiple .... [1]
 (a) unknown variables, goals seek (b) variables, equation
 (c) goal seek, unknown variables (d) subtotal, goal seek

(iv) Template includes .... text that is surrounded by brackets. [1]
 (a) margin   (b) placeholder
 (c) data source   (d) track changes

(v) In the Load Style dialog box, option loads the paragraph and the character styles from the selected document into the current document. [1]
 (a) Page (b) Paragraph (c) Overwrite (d) Text

(vi) Which of the following is an attribute whose value is derived from the primary key of some other table? [1]
 (a) Primary key   (b) Foreign key
 (c) Alternate key   (d) None of these

3. Answer any 5 out of the given 6 questions [1 × 5 = 5 Marks]

(i) The status of your document like current page number and number of pages are given by .... [1]
 (a) Formatting toolbar   (b) Status bar
 (c) Standard toolbar   (d) None of these

(ii) A tuple in RDBMS is referred to .... of a table. [1]
    (a) record   (b) field
    (c) table   (d) key

(iii) Which client software is used to request and display web pages? ....is used to transfer files between computers on a network. [1]
    (a) Web server   (b) FTP
    (c) Multimedia   (d) Web browser

(iv) Editing Custom Shapes feature allows .... of small segments of a drawing. [1]
    (a) shaping   (b) reshaping
    (c) rehearse   (d) None of these

(v) .... function takes data from a series of worksheets or workbooks and summaries it into a single worksheet that you can update easily. [1]
    (a) Summation   (b) Data Consolidation
    (c) Data Format   (d) Data Chart

(vi) Which tab is used to share the worksheet data? [1]
    (a) Home   (b) Review   (c) Insert   (d) Layout

4. Answer any 5 out of the given 6 questions   [1 × 5 = 5 Marks]

(i) To join the Internet, the computer has to be connected to a [1]
    (a) Internet Architecture Board   (b) Internet society
    (c) Internet Service Provider   (d) None of these

(ii) By dragging any .... handle you can increase or decrease the .... of the image diagonally. [1]
    (a) comer, size   (b) side, quality
    (c) top, depth   (d) comer, quality

(iii) Key field is a unique identifier for each record. It is defined in the form of [1]
    (a) rows   (b) columns
    (c) tree   (d) query

(iv) Wireless broadband can be [1]
    (a) mobile   (b) fixed
    (c) Both (a) and (b)   (d) None of these

(v) A relational database is a collection of [1]
    (a) attributes   (b) tables   (c) records   (d) fields

(vi) .... ensure that all the documents have a standard layout, look and feel. [1]
    (a) Graphics   (b) Layout
    (c) Properties   (d) Templates

5. Answer any 5 out of the given 6 questions   [1 × 5 = 5 Marks]

(i) .... determines the range of field values. [1]
    (a) Field Name   (b) Data Type
    (c) Field Size   (d) Description

(ii) Rajat has received a spreadsheet, which is reviewed by his subordinates Puneet, Kavya and Aman, who made some corrections in it. Before Rajat shared the spreadsheet with his subordinates, he has activated the track changes feature. Which of the following option he should use now to keep some of the changes made by them? [1]
    (a) Accept and reject changes   (b) Overwrite and keep changes
    (c) Both (a) and (b)   (d) None of these

(iii) Computer based record keeping system is known as   [1]
    (a) Data Manipulation System   (b) Computerised Data System
    (c) Computerised Record Keeping System (d) DBMS

(iv) Which of the following is an AutoShape?   [1]
    (a) Line   (b) Circle
    (c) Curve   (d) All of these

(v) Which type of hazard can cause skin irritation, illness or breathing problems?   [1]
    (a) Chemical hazard   (b) Biological hazard
    (c) Slipping hazard   (d) None of these

(vi) If you have unsafe and unhealthy workplace, there will be higher days lost and will have higher   [1]
    (a) employee satisfaction   (b) productivity
    (c) stress levels   (d) None of these

Section-B

(Subjective Type Questions)

- Answer any 3 out of the given 5 questions on Employability skills.   [2 × 3 = 6 Marks]
- Answer each question in 20-30 words.

6. Why is communication important? What are its types? How can you deal with it?   [2]

7. What do you mean by survival stress?   [2]

8. Explain the use of Disk Defragmenter.   [2]

9. Name two basic elements of entrepreneurship.   [2]

10. Sustainable forest management was developed in Europe during which centuries?   [2]

- Answer any 4 out of the given 6 questions in 20-30 words each.   [2 × 4 = 8 Marks]

11. How to add a comment in a word processor application?   [2]

12. Write the steps to sort the data in a worksheet.   [2]

13. Mention any two string data types in database.   [2]

14. Mention any two components of a database.   [2]

15. When the computer network uses telephone lines as communication channel, then MODEM is used as a data communication device. Now, explain the working of MODEM.   [2]

16. Define the following :   [2]
    (i) Peer-to-Peer architecture   (ii) Internet

- Answer any 3 out of the given 5 questions in 50-80 words each.   [4 × 3 = 12 Marks]

17. Manisha had created a Table of Contents of the project done by her. Tell her the different steps to do the following: [4]

(a) Creating a TOC   (b) Deleting a TOC

18. Simran wants to add macro in a spreadsheet application. Tell her the different steps involved in adding a macro.   [4]

19. Consider the following table ITEM NAMES :   [4]

S_No	P_Name	S_Name	Qty	Cost	City
S1	Biscuit	Priyagold	120	12.00	Delhi
S2	Bread	Britannia	200	25.00	Mumbai
S3	Chocolate	Cadbury	350	40.00	Mumbai
S4	Sauce	Kissan	400	45.00	Chennai

(i) How many records and fields in the table ITEM NAMES?

(ii) Write the SQL queries for

(a) Display all the products whose quantity in between 100 and 350.

(b) Display the data for all products sorted by their quantity.

(c) To list S_Name, P_Name, Cost for all the products whose quantity is less than 400.

20. Answer the following questions regarding database: [4]

(i) Mention any two databases.

(ii) Define different forms of a database.

(iii) What is an attribute whose value is derived from the primary key of some other table?

(iv) Define the SELECT command.

21. Riya is a student of class X. She had heard about network devices. She had some queries. Help her by answering her queries.   [4]

(i) What is network device?

(ii) Name any two network devices.

(iii) Which device is used as proxy server?

(iv) What is the basic function of repeater?

Answers

1. (i)(b), (ii)(d), (iii)(b), (iv)(a), (v)(b), (vi)(a)

2. (i)(b), (ii)(a), (iii)(c), (iv)(b), (v)(d), (vi)(c)

3. (i)(b), (ii)(a), (iii)(b), (iv)(b), (v)(b), (vi)(b)

4. (i)(c), (ii)(a), (iii)(b), (iv)(c), (v)(b), (vi)(d)

5. (i)(c), (ii)(a), (iii)(d), (iv)(d), (v)(a), (vi)(c)

Answers to the
Qualifying R⊖und

Unit-1 : Communication Skills-II

1. oral, written

2. interjection

3. The predicate part of a sentence includes the verb and the words that relate to it. It tells what the subject does with an action verb or describes the subject.

4. Encoding a message means to change the message into a form suitable for sending. The factors which must be considered when encoding messages are language, cultural differences etc.

5. (i) **Transmission of message** describes one-way, linear process in which a sender encodes a message and transmits it through a channel to a receiver who decodes it. The transmission of message may be distrupted by environmental or semantic noise.

  (ii) **Feedback** is the receiver's response to the message. Requesting clarification is part of a good feedback phase of a communication cycle. Without feedback, the communication cycle remains incomplete.

6. Semantics barriers refer to symbols or visuals used in the message. The barrier may arise due to the symbol we use, as it may mean different things to different people. For example, the 'thumbs up' gesture is recognised as a sign of approval or agreement in European countries, but it may be interpreted as an indecent gesture in rural areas of India.

7. Differences between specific feedback and non-specific feedback are follows

Specific Feedback	Non-specific Feedback
Specific feedback describes specific information of a message.	Non-specific feedback gives overall feedback and does not mention anything specific.
e.g. • I like the way you described your grandfather. It makes me feel like I know him too. • I like the part where you fell. It made me laugh. • I like the part where you and your sister were fighting. I fight with my brother too.	**e.g.** • I like your story. It's good. • I like your topic. I want to write about that too. • I like the ending. It was different than I expected.

8. To ensure that barriers to communication do not arise or can be overcome, we can take some steps related to the factors causing the barriers. The steps to be taken for overcoming some of these factors are:

  (i) Be prepared before communicating

  (ii) Give sufficient time

  (iii) Simplify the language

  (iv) Don't assume anything

  (v) Avoid overconfidence

  (vi) Preconceived notions/expectations, perceptions and assumptions

  (vii) Avoid making judgements

  (viii) Respect the receiver

  (ix) Improve the attitude

  (x) Information overload/ attention span

9. We communicate at home, at work, with our neighbour etc. We communicate in written or oral, audio or visual, so it is important that we follow the 7C's of effective communication.

   These principles of effective communication are:

   (i) Completeness   (ii) Conciseness

   (iii) Consideration   (iv) Concreteness

   (v) Clarity   (vi) Courtesy

   (vii) Correctness

10. A sentence consists of two parts, a **subject part** and a **predicate part**. Each part of a sentence has a particular function, though sometimes both parts may not be written for it to be complete. The subject refers to that part of the sentence which tells who or what the sentence is about. The subject is a noun, pronoun or noun phrase. Instances of typical sentences with such subjects are:

    - Kailash ran across the road.   ('Kailash' is a noun)

    The predicate part of a sentence includes the verb and the words that relate to it. It tells what the subject does with an action verb or describes the subject. Predicates can contain much information and may be quite long. Predicates often have several parts in addition to the verb, including objects and complements. Instances of predicates are underlined in the sentences given below:

    - The letter <u>contained exciting news.</u>

Unit-2 : Self-Management Skills-II

1. Self-regulation

2. Internal stress

3. Leisure gives the benefits by enabling a person to indulge in his/her interests, hobbies, gives them a break and provides an outlet for relief.

4. The type of personality determines to a large extent what causes stress in us. For example, if we are overambitious and set an unrealistically high goal for ourselves in any activity we undertake, we will definitely become likely to have a stress related physical problem. Other persons, who do not set such high goals, will achieve their goals. Thus, they will not have any stress related problems.

5. **Fight-or-flight** is a common response to danger in all people and animals. When you are afraid that someone or something may physically hurt you, your body automatically responds with a burst of energy so that you will be better able to survive the dangerous situation (i.e. fight) or escape it altogether (i.e. flight). This is termed as the 'fight-or-flight response'.

6. In meditation, we change from our normal activities to silence. We go beyond the noisy thoughts in the mind and enter a state of restful alertness. During meditation, although we are in a state of deep rest, our mind is fully alert and awake. At this time, the body experiences many healing effects which are the reverse of the 'fight-or-flight' response, such as decreased heart rate, normalisation of blood pressure, deeper breathing, reduced production of stress hormones, higher immunity, more efficient use of oxygen by the body and reduced inflammation.

7. **The Alarm Response** is when body responds to a stressful situation by pumping adrenalin so that the muscles become tense and the heart rate increases. Mostly, this causes distress, although we can also respond calmly to such situations. Everyone is different, with their unique reactions to events. There is no single level of stress that is optimal for all people. Some are more sensitive than others due to experiences in childhood, the influence of teachers, parents, religion etc.

8. Some skills are required for developing an independent working style. These are:
   - Becoming self-aware, self-monitoring and self-correcting.
   - Knowing what we need to do.
   - Taking the initiative rather than waiting to be told what to do.
   - Doing what is asked to the best of our ability, without the need for external prodding and working until the job is completed.
   - Learning to work at a pace that we can sustain for a long time.
   - Taking ownership of our mistakes without looking for excuses.
   - Refusing to let self-doubt or negative emotions due to negative past experiences take us away from the task.

   Thus, the key to being independent is our self-awareness, self-motivation and self-regulation.

9. Stress can result due to stimulus from external factors such as environment and social factors or internal factors such as fatigue, emotions or illness.

   On the basis of stimulus, stress may be classified into four types:

   (i) **Survival Stress** When you are afraid that someone may physically hurt you, your body automatically responds with a burst of energy so that you will be better able to survive the dangerous situation or escape it altogether. This is known as survival stress.

   (ii) **Internal Stress** It generates within the human regarding the unreasonable matters. This internal stress is one of the most important kind of stress to understand and manage because it keeps on building up as time passes.

   (iii) **Environmental Stress** It is a response to happenings around us that cause stress such as noise, pollution, family tensions, etc. Some of these may be under our control if we try to control them, whereas some may not be controllable by us.

   (iv) **Fatigue Related Stress** This kind of stress builds up over a long time. It can be caused by working too long or too hard at our job. It can also be caused by exercising too much or too long. If a person does not know how to manage his time well, then he will become a victim of fatigue related stress.

10. Self-awareness refers to our knowledge and understanding of ourselves. It includes our emotions, beliefs, assumptions, biases, knowledge base, abilities, motivations, interests etc., So, we should make a conscious effort to learn about ourselves, i.e. our abilities, beliefs, likes and dislikes. The feeling of self-awareness enhances our self-confidence.

    There are four kinds of self-awareness. These are:

    1. **About Your Strengths** To find out your strengths, find out what you like to do, what you are enthusiastic about doing and what work done by you is given good comments by others.

    2. **About Your Weaknesses** If you know what you find difficult to do or cannot do, you can ask other people to help you in that task. Otherwise you can remove this weakness by learning that particular task.

    3. **About Your Flaws** You should not hide your flaws but take other people's help in overcoming them.

    4. **About Your Emotional Problems** A typical emotional problem is getting angry on small matters. Such emotional problems in your character should be kept under control when some incident triggers them.

Unit-3 : Basic ICT Skills-II

1. Word wrap

2. Spreadsheet

3. **Save a Presentation**

   Choose File > Save As from the menu bar. Select the location where you want the PowerPoint file saved and type a name for the file.

   Print a presentation

   (i) Select File > Print.

   (ii) For Printer, select the printer you want to print to.

   (iii) For Settings, select the options you want:

   • Print All Slides: To print each slide on a single sheet or change to just print a range of slides.

   • Slides: From the drop-down, choose to print all slides, selected slides, or the current slide. Or, in the Slides box, type which slide numbers to print, separated by a comma.

   (iv) For Copies, select how many copies you want to print.

   (v) Select Print.

4. (i) Choose Format > Styles and Formatting, right click on Default and choose Modify > Font.

   To change an existing style using the Style dialog, right-click on the required style in the Styles and Formatting window and select Modify from the pop-up menu. The Style dialog displayed depends on the type of style selected. Each style dialog has several tabs.

   (ii) Formulas are equations using numbers and variables to get a result. In a spreadsheet, the variables are cell locations that hold the data needed for the equation to be completed. A function is a predefined calculation entered in a cell to help you analyze or manipulate data in a spreadsheet. All you have to do is add the arguments, and the calculation is automatically made for you. Functions help you create the formulas needed to get the results that you are looking for.

5. **Step 1** Open the document by double-clicking on the icon on the desktop or in the appropriate folder. If it prompts you for a password, enter it.

   Step 2 Click "File" and "Save As." Choose the option that saves the file with the ".xlt" extension. Uncheck the option in the bottom left corner that says "Save with password." Press "Save." This removes the password protection.

   Step 3 Click the "Tools" menu and choose "Protect Document." Either the "Sheet" or "Document" option may have a checkmark next to it. Uncheck it. You may need to enter the password. This will unprotect the entire document. Verify this by typing in one of the cells. If you can type in the cells, they are unprotected. Save by pressing "Ctrl+s."

6. A word processor is a computer program used to create and print text documents. It is an application that allows to type in, edit, format, save and print text. The key advantage of a word processor is its ability to make changes easily such as correcting spelling, adding, deleting, formatting and relocating text.

   The software packages that are helpful to learn about word processing are Microsoft Word, Open Office Writer, Corel WordPerfect, Apple Pages and Google Docs (Internet based).

7. The Find and Replace feature helps us to replace a particular text with different text wherever necessary in the entire document.

   To display the Find and Replace dialog box, use the keyboard shortcut Control+F or select Edit > Find and Replace.

   (i) Type the text you want to find in the Search for box.

   (ii) To replace the text with different text, type the new text in the Replace with box.

   (iii) You can select various options, such as matching the case, matching whole words only, or doing a search for similar words. (See below for some other choices.)

   (iv) When you have set up your search, click Find. To replace text, click Replace instead.

8. Slide transitions are the effects that take place when one slide gives way to the next one in the presentation, like Roll down from top or Fly in from left. They add dynamic flair to a slideshow, smoothing the transition between slides.

   You can add transitions while in Slide Sorter view or in Normal view. To see the effect of a selection, you need to be in Normal view and select the Automatic preview checkbox on the Slide Transition page of the Tasks pane.

   You can apply a single type of transition to all slides in the presentation or apply a different transition to any single slide

   Slide animations are similar to transitions, but they are applied to individual elements on a single slide—a title, chart, image, or individual bullet point. Animations can make a presentation more lively and memorable. Just as with transitions, heavy use of animations can be fun, but distracting and even annoying for an audience expecting a professional presentation.

   Animation effects need to be applied from Normal View so that you can select individual objects on a single slide.

9. Impress is a truly outstanding tool for creating effective multimedia presentations. The presentations stand out with 2D and 3D clip art, special effects, animation, and high-impact drawing tools.

   - Master Pages simplify the task of preparing your materials. Readymade templates can be easily downloaded.
   - Complete range of Views are supported: Slides / Outline / Notes / Handouts to meet all the needs of presenters and audiences, plus an optional multi-pane view to put all the tools at your fingertips.
   - Multiple monitors support so that presenters can have additional materials or notes while presenting their slides on a projector. An integrated Presenter Screen, lets you see your next slides as well as the time and the speaker notes.
   - Easy-to-use drawing and diagramming tools - a complete range to add up to your presentation. 'Park' your most commonly used drawing tools around your screen ready for single-click access.
   - Slide show Animation and Effects bring your presentation to life. Fontworks provides stunning 2D and 3D images from text. Create lifelike 3D images with astounding speed and response.
   - .odp Standard - Save your presentations in OpenDocument format, the new international standard for office documents. This XML based format means you're not tied up with using Impress. You can access your presentations from any OpenDocument compliant software.
   - .ppt and .pptx support - Of course, you are free to import your old Microsoft PowerPoint presentations, or save your work in PowerPoint format for sending to people who are still using Microsoft products.
   - Flash .swf support - Alternatively, use Impress's built-in ability to create Flash versions of your presentations.

10. There are several ways to insert a new sheet. The first step for all of the methods is to select the sheet that the new sheet will be inserted next to. Then any of the following options can be used.

- Click on the Insert menu and select Sheet, or
- Right-click on its tab and select Insert Sheet, or
- Click into an empty space at the end of the line of sheet tabs.

Each method opens the Insert Sheet dialog. Here you can select whether the new sheet is to go before or after the selected sheet and how many sheets you want to insert. If you are inserting only one sheet, there is the opportunity to give the sheet a name.

Features of Open Office Calc

(i) **Connecting with Excel** Ability to open, edit, and save Microsoft Excel spreadsheets.

(ii) **AutoSum** Helps you to add the contents of a cluster of adjacent cells.

(iii) **List AutoFill** Automatically extends cell formatting when a new item is added to the end of a list.

(iv) **AutoFill** Allows you to quickly fill cells with repetitive or sequential data such as chronological dates or numbers, and repeated text. AutoFill can also be used to copy functions. You can also alter text and numbers with this feature.

Unit-4 : Entrepreneurship Skills-II

1. employment

2. Leadership, Risk taking

3. An entrepreneur is an individual who creates a new business, bearing most of the risks and enjoying most of the rewards.

- Entrepreneurship refers to the functions performed by an entrepreneur. It is the process involving various actions to be undertaken by the entrepreneur in establishing a new enterprise.

4. Two functions of an entrepreneur are as follows :

- **Innovation** It includes introducing new products, opening new markets, new sources of raw material and new organisation structure.
- **Risk-Taking** An entrepreneur has to take risk by choosing one among various alternatives.

5. For the successful enterprise, it is important to understand the characteristics/quality of successful entrepreneurs and it is described below :

- **Leadership** An entrepreneur must possess the characteristics of leadership and must lead a team for achievement of goals. The leader is able to clearly articulate their ideas and has a clear vision. An entrepreneurial leader realises the importance of initiative and reactiveness and they go out of their way to provide a support to the team.
- **Risk Taking** An entrepreneur with rational planning and firm decisions bear the risks. They have differentiated approach towards risks. Good entrepreneurs are always ready to invest their time and money but they always have a back up for every risk they take.
- **Innovativeness** With the changing needs and requirements of customers production should meet requirements with the help of innovative ideas. An entrepreneurial venture does not have to restrict itself to just one innovation or even one type of innovation. Success can be built on combination of innovation for example, a new product delivered in a new way with a new message.
- **Goal-oriented** Goal-oriented entrepreneurs achieve the maximum results from their efforts in business due to the fact they work towards clear and measurable targets.

6. The role and significance of entrepreneurs are as follows :

- **Organiser of Society's Productive Resources** An entrepreneur is the organiser of society's productive resources. He is the person who assembles the unused natural, physical and human resources of the society, combines them as properly, establishes effective coordination between them and makes the economic activities dynamic.
- **Helpful in Capital Formation** An entrepreneur is helpful in capital formation as we know that increase in the rate of capital formation is quite essential for the economic development of any country. Those nations which are not able to increase the rate of capital formation or does it nominally remain backward from industrial development's point of view.

- **Increase in Employment Opportunities** An entrepreneur creates maximum employment opportunities in the society by way of establishing new industries, developing and expanding the existing industries and by undertaking innovative activities.
- **Development of New Production Techniques** An entrepreneur does not feel contended only with the existing techniques of production. Hence, he carries out various experiments for saving time, labour and capital in the production, as also to improve the variety and quality of the product and service.
- **Visionary Leader** An entrepreneur has a good vision towards the achievement of his goals. He is able to recognise profitable opportunities and conceptualise strategies.

7. The main advantages of adopting entrepreneurship as a career are discussed below :
   - **Independence** An entrepreneur is himself a boss or owner and he can take all the decisions independently.
   - **Excitement** Entrepreneurship can be very exciting with many entrepreneurs considering their ventures highly enjoyable. Everyday will be filled with new opportunities to challenge your determination, skills and abilities.
   - **Wealth Creation** The principal focus of entrepreneurship is wealth creation and improved livelihood by means of making available goods and services. Entrepreneurial venture generates new wealth, new and improved products, services or technology form entrepreneurs, enable new markets to be developed and new wealth to be created.
   - **Flexibility** As an entrepreneur you can schedule your work hours around other commitments, including quality time you would spend with your family.
   - **Status** Success in entrepreneurship beings a considerable fame and prestige within the society.

8. Some of the disadvantages of entrepreneurship are as follows :
   - **Uncertain Income** There is no regular or fixed income available to an entrepreneur. So, there is uncertain kind of income received by an entrepreneur.
   - **Incompetent Staff** A new entrepreneur may not be able to hire qualified and experienced staff so there are chances of incompetency by the staff due to lack of experience and knowledge.

9. • **Increase in Employment Opportunities** An entrepreneur creates maximum employment opportunities in the society by way of establishing new industries, developing and expanding the existing industries and by undertaking innovative activities.
   - **Development of New Production Techniques** An entrepreneur does not feel contended only with the existing techniques of production. Hence, he carries out various experiments for saving time, labour and capital in the production, as also to improve the variety and quality of the product and service.

10. Many entrepreneurs believe a set of myths about entrepreneurship and the most common are as follows :
   - **Starting a Business is Easy** In reality, it is a very difficult and challenging process to start a successful business. The rate of failure of new ventures is very high but small entrepreneurships are comparatively easier to start.
   - **Lot of Money to Finance New Business** Successful entrepreneurs design their business with little cash also.
   - **Start up's cannot be Financed** Under the schemes like MUDRA, entrepreneurs can raise loans from banks.
   - **Talent is More Important than Industry** This is not true as the nature of industry an entrepreneur chooses greatly effects the success and growth of the business.

Unit-5 : Green Skills-II

1. Deforestation, afforestation

2. renewable

3. Brundtland Report defined sustainable development as, "Development that meets the needs of the present, without compromising the ability of future generation to meet their needs."

4. The two challenges to sustainable development are:
   (i) Rise in population level would lead to severe environmental degradation in the future.
   (ii) Poor management of natural resources combined with growing economic activities will continue to pose serious challenges to environment.

5. The achievement of sustainable development requires the integration of economic, environmental and social components at all levels.

6. Sustainable development is necessary for the maintenance of the environment.

   There is a need of sustainable development because of the following reasons:
   (i) Sustainable development teaches people to make use of means and resources for the maximum benefit without wastage.
   (ii) Sustainable development brings about changes in people's knowledge, attitude and skill.
   (iii) Sustainable development aims at achieving the goal of economic and social development without destroying the Earth's means and resources.

7. The short-term solutions to sustainable development are as follows:
   (i) The practice of illegal deforestation and smuggling of forest resources should be stopped.
   (ii) Proper balance ought to be maintained between deforestation and afforestation.
   (iii) Planning and building of industrial zones to manage and process are types of wastes.
   (iv) Proper treatment system, recycling of waste and their proper disposal should be undertaken.
   (v) Adoption of rainwater harvesting techniques, drip/sprinkler irrigation and use of alternative sources of energy.
   (vi) Less chemical fertilizers should be used along with environment friendly pesticides and weedicides.

8. **United Nations Sustainable Development Summit (2015)** sets global development goals. These goals are termed as Agenda 2030. The goals are:
   1. End poverty in all forms everywhere.
   2. End hunger, achieve food security and improved nutrition and promote **sustainable agriculture**.
   3. Ensure healthy lives and well-being for all.
   4. Ensure inclusive and quality education for all and promote lifelong learning.
   5. Achieve gender equality and empower all women and girls.
   6. Ensure access to water and sanitation for all.
   7. Ensure access to affordable, reliable, sustainable and modern energy for all.
   8. Promote inclusive and sustainable economic growth, employment and decent work for all.
   9. Build resilient infrastructure, promote sustainable industrialisation and foster innovation.
   10. Reduce inequality within and among countries.

9. **Problems related to sustainable development**
   - Poor management of natural resources combined with growing economic activities will continue to pose serious challenges to environment.
   - The most significant environmental problems are associated with resources that are renewable such as air and water. They have finite capacity to assimilate emissions and wastes but if pollution exceeds this capacity ecosystem can deteriorate rapidly.
   - To assess the regenerative capacity of natural resources is difficult to determine. In the cases of soil erosion, atmospheric pollution etc., there is substantial uncertainity about the extent and outcomes of environmental degradation.
   - The overall effects of economic activities on the environment are continuously changing.

   Solutions related to sustainable development
   - Inspite of difficult circumstances sustainable development is achievable however, it would require a lots of concentrated and coordinated effort. The achievement of sustainable development requires the integration of economic, environmental and social components at all levels.

   The main principles of sustainable development are:
   - Respect and care for all forms of life.
   - People should learn to conserve the natural resoures in order to protect the living beings.
   - Conserving the Earth's vitality and diversity.
   - Improving the quality of human life.
   - Changing personal attitude and practices towards the environment.

10. Sustainable development is necessary for the maintenance of the environment. The importance of sustainable development are as follows:
   - **Proper Use of Means and Resources** Sustainable development teaches people to make use of means and resources for the maximum benefit without wastage. It helps to conserve and promote the environment.
   - **Development of Positive Attitude** Sustainable development brings about changes in people's knowledge, attitude and skills. It awares the people the responsibility to use and preserve natural resources. It creates the feeling that natural resources are the common property of all and nobody can use the property according to his personal will. It helps to conserve natural and social environment.
   - **Development Based on People's Participation** People's participation is to be given priority in development work in order to achieve the aim of sustainable development. It creates the interest of local people in development work and environment conservation with the feeling of ownership.
   - **Limitation of Development** Limited but effective use of means and resources are enough for the people to satisfy their basic needs. Limited and non-renewable means and resources go on decreasing in globally due to over-use. Development works should be conducted as per carrying capacity.
   - **Long Lasting Development** Sustainable development aims at achieving the goal of economic and social development without destroying the Earth's means and resources. It attempts to create the concept of maintaining the present work for the future and conserving the natural resources for future generation.

Part B Subject Skills

Unit-1 : Digital Documentation (Advanced)

1. Justify

2. header, footer

3. To insert text into a template, we should follow given steps:

   Step 1 Click near the text that we want to replace. The text will be highlighted and a template tag will appear.

   Step 2 Enter text. It will replace placeholder text with our entered text.

4. Difference between odd page break and even page break is that odd page break will insert a section break into your Word document that will break to the next odd page in the Word document while even page break will insert a section break into your Word document that happens on every even page of your Word document.

5. Five items that can be added to the header section of a document can be :
   (i)   The title of the document
   (ii) Name of the document
   (iii) Pic/logo for the document
   (iv) Menu (that contain home, about, services etc.)
   (v)   Date and time

6. The word processor object allows different formatting within the same object. However, word processor objects are printed as an image, so they require quite a bit more resources than a normal single or multiline text objects. Word processing objects includes text, graphical and embedded objects.

7. There are five text case options as follows:
   (i)   **Sentence case** It is used to change the first letter of every sentence in uppercase.
   (ii) **Lowercase** It changes the whole selected text in lowercase letters.
   (iii) **Uppercase** It changes the whole selected text in uppercase letters.
   (iv) **Capitalise Each Word** It is used to change first letter of every word in capital case.
   (v)   **Togglecase** It toggles whole selected text, i.e., changes each capital letter into lowercase and each small letter into uppercase.

8. • You can right-click on a word with a wavy underline, to open a context menu. If you select from the suggested words on the menu, the selection will replace the misspelled word in your text.
   • You can change the dictionary language (for example, to Spanish, French or German) on the Spelling dialog box.
   • You can add a word to the dictionary. Click Add in the Spelling dialog box and pick the dictionary to add it to.

- The Options dialog of the Spelling tool has a number of different options, such as whether to check uppercase words and words with numbers. It also allows you to manage custom dictionaries; that is, add or delete dictionaries, and add or delete words in a dictionary.

9. An important part of creating effective documents lies in the document design. Line spacing or paragraph spacing is measured in lines or points, which is referred to as leading. As a part of designing, the document and making formatting decisions, you will need to know how to modify the spacing. Just as you can format spacing between lines in your document, you can also choose spacing options between each paragraph.

   Typically, extra spaces are added between paragraphs, headings or subheadings. Extra spacing between paragraphs adds emphasis and makes a document easier to read. When you reduce the leading, you automatically bring the lines of text closer together. Increasing the leading will space the lines out, allowing for improved readability.

10. To resize an image:
    1. Click one time on the image to select it.
    2. From the Menu bar select: Format ? Position and Size.
    3. Choose the Position & Size tab.
    4. Insert the desired image size and click the OK button.

    Or

    1. Click one time on the image to select it. Little green squares will appear around the image.
    2. Drag one of the squares to resize the image.

Unit-2 : Electronic Spreadsheet (Advanced)

1. Absolute, relative, mixed

2. Scenarios

3. Using the workbook views group of commands, you can view your Excel workbook in different layouts. Five types of views. i.e. Normal, Page Layout, Page Break Preview, Custom Views and Full Screen are available in spreadsheet.

4. Cell referencing in which the cells are referred by their relative position in the worksheet relative to a particular cell is called relative referencing.

   Formula for adding values of cells A1 to A5 would be = SUM(A1 : A5)

5. To keep an area of a worksheet visible while you scroll to another area of the worksheet, go to the View tab, where you can freeze panes to lock specific rows and columns in place, or you can split panes to create separate window of the same worksheet.

6. Pie charts are useful for the following purposes:
   (i)   They convey approximate propositional relationship at a point in time.
   (ii) They compare part of a whole at a given point in time.
   (iii) Exploded portion of a pie chart emphasise a small proportion of part.

7. The chart elements are as follows :
   (i)   **X-axis** is a horizontal axis known as category axis.
   (ii) **Y-axis** is a vertical axis known as value axis.
   (iii) **Data Series** is the set of values you want to plot in the chart.
   (iv) **Chart Area** is the total area of the chart.
   (v)   **Chart Title** is the descriptive text aimed at helping user to identify the chart.
   (vi) **Gridlines** are horizontal and vertical lines which are inserted in the chart.
   (vii) **Data Label** provides additional information about a data marker.

8. To identify duplicates :
   1. Select the cells you want to check for duplicates.
   2. Click Home > Format > Conditional Formatting > Highlight Cells Rules > Duplicate Values.
   3. In the box next to values with, pick the formatting you want to apply to the duplicate values, and then click OK.

9. The workbook views options allow user to view or see the spreadsheet differently. You can adjust the excel window to suit what you are currently working on by changing the view to match your current task.

   There are five types of view available in the spreadsheet.

(i) **Normal** This is the default view of the spreadsheet application. Normal view is used for building and editing the worksheets.

(ii) **Page Layout** It displays worksheets as they would appear if you printed them out. Through this option, you can check from where the page begin and end as well as to see the header/footer on the page.

(iii) **Page Break Preview** You can use this option to see where the page breaks appear when you print the document. It displays the page breaks as blue line.

(iv) **Custom Views** You can use this option to save the current by display document and setting as a custom view which you can apply in future. It allows you to save specific display settings and print settings for a worksheet.

(v) **Full Screen** It displays only the worksheet, no formula bar, ribbon or status bar are visible. This allows you to maximise the amount of content you see in your worksheet.

10. Open the Calc document where the external data is to be inserted. This is the target document. 2) Select the cell where the upper left-hand cell of the external data is to be inserted. 3) Choose Insert > Link to External Data. 4) On the External Data dialog, type the URL of the source document or click the [...] button to open a file selection dialog. Press Enter to get Calc to load the list of available tables. 5) In the Available tables/range list, select the named ranges or tables you want to insert. You can also specify that the ranges or tables are updated every n seconds. 6) Click OK to save and close this dialog.

Using the Navigator

(i) Open the OpenOffice.org Calc spreadsheet in which the external data is to be inserted (target document).

(ii) Open the document from which the external data is to be taken (source document). Choose Web Page Query (OpenOffice.org Calc) as the file type.

(iii) In the target document, open the Navigator.

(iv) At the bottom of the Navigator, select the source document. The Navigator now shows the range names or the tables contained in the source document (the example contains range names; other documents have a list of tables). Click on the + next to Range names to display the list.

(v) In the Navigator, select the Insert as Link drag mode.

(vi) Select the required range or table and drag it from the Navigator into the target document, to the cell where you want the upper left-hand cell of the data range to be Selecting a data range in a source document, to be inserted as a link 7) In the target document, check the Navigator. Instead of a + by Range names, it shows a + by Linked areas. Click the + to see the same range name.

Unit-3 : Database Management System

1. Candidate key

2. Memo

3. Differences between DDL and DML :

DDL	DML
DDL is the abbreviation of Data Definition Language.	DML is the abbreviation of Data Manipulation Language.
It is used to create and modify the structure of database objects in database.	It is used to retrieve, store, modify, delete, insert and update data in database.
DDL commands allow us to perform tasks related to data definition.	DML commands are used to manipulate data.
For example, CREATE, ALTER, and DROP commands.	For example, SELECT, UPDATE, and INSERT commands.

4. There are two kinds of user in the schema :

- **Users** They work with the data, but cannot change the structure of the schema. They write data manipulation language.

- **Admin** They can change the structure of the schema and control access to the schema objects. They write data definition language.

5. Some rules for creating tables are as follows:

(i) The table and column names must start with a letter and can be followed by letters, numbers, or underscores.

(ii) Table or column names not to exceed a total of 30 characters in length and not use any SQL reserved keywords as names for tables or column names (such as 'select', 'create', 'insert', etc).

(iii) It is important to make sure that you are using an open parenthesis before the beginning of a table definition and a closing parenthesis after the end of the last column definition.

(iv) Separate each column definition with a comma (,).

(v) All SQL statements should end with a semi-colon (;).

6. **Relationship between primary key and foreign key :**

A foreign key is a column or set of columns in one table that references the primary key columns in another table.

Difference between primary key and foreign key :

Primary key can't accept null values whereas foreign key can accept multiple null value.

7. (i) **AutoNumber** It allows to store numbers that are automatically generated for each record. It increases the number automatically.

(ii) **Currency** It allows to store monetary values that can be used in calculations accurate upto 15 digits on LHS and 4 digits on RHS of decimal points.

(iii) **Text** It allows to store text or combination of text and numbers, as well as numbers that don't require calculations such as phone numbers.

8. Queries are a way to get specific information from the database. They give us the ability to ask questions record them for later and to take action on answers.

9. Distinguish between a record and a field in a table are as follows:

Record	Field
• It is a collection of data items which represent a complete unit of information about a thing or a person.	It is an area with in the record reserved for a specific piece of data.
• A record refers to a row in the table.	A field refers to a column in the table.
• Record is also known as tuple.	Field is also known as attribute.
• e.g. If Employee is a table, then entire information of an employee is called a record.	e.g. If Employee is a table, then empld, empName, department, Salary are the fields.

10. The advantages of using a database management system in a hospital are :

(i) It stores data about all the doctors patients, departments of a hospital.

(ii) It provides security to the personal information of the hospital stored in it.

DML provides various commands used to access and manipulate data in existing database. This manipulation involves inserting data into database tables, retrieving existing data, deleting data from existing tables and modifying existing data.

DML is mostly incorporated in SQL database. The basic goal of DML is to provide efficient human interaction with the system.

The DMLs are of two types :

Procedural DMLs These require a user to specify what data is needed and how to get it.

Non-Procedural DMLs These require a user to specify what data is needed without specifying how to get it.

Various data manipulation language commands are as follows :

(i) **SELECT** Used to retrieve data from a database.

(ii) **INSERT** Used to insert data into a table.

(iii) **UPDATE** Used to update existing data within a table.

(iv) **DELETE** Used to delete all records from a table, the space of the records remains.

(v) **LOCK TABLE** Used to control concurrency.

A query language is a portion of a DML involving information retrieval only. The terms DML and query language are often used synonymously.

Unit-4 : Web Applications and Security

1. PAN (Personal Area Network)

2. Web based

3. URL

4. A computer networking is the practice for exchanging information/services between two or more computers together for the purpose of sharing data.

Following are the three main types of computer networks, based upon the geographical area as follows:

(i) Local Area Network (LAN)　　　　　　(ii) Metropolitan Area Network (MAN)

(iii) Wide Area Network (WAN)

5. (i) **Router** A device that is used to connect different types of networks. It performs the necessary translation so that the connected networks can communicate properly.

(ii) **Modem** A device that converts data from digital bit stream into an analog signal and vice-versa.

6. Four advantages of networking are as follows :

(i) **User Communication** Network allows users to communicate using emails, social networking sites, video conferencing, etc.

(ii) **File Sharing** By using networking, data or information can be shared or transferred from one computer to another.

(iii) **Media and Entertainment** Most of the companies and TV channels use network to broadcast audio and video including live radio and television programmes.

(iv) **Hardware Sharing** Hardware components such as printers, scanners, etc., can also be shared. For example, instead of purchasing 10 printers, one printer can be purchased and shared among multiple users thus, saving cost.

7. Differences between circuit switching and packet switching are as follows :

Circuit Switching	Packet Switching
Initially designed for voice communication.	Initially designed for data transmission.
Inflexible, because once a path is set all parts of a transmission follows the same path.	Flexible, because a route is created for each packet to travel to the destination.
It is connection oriented.	It is connectionless.

In a network, repeater receives a weak signal coming from a source and amplifies it to its original strength and then again forwards it to the destination. Basically, repeaters are used in a network so that a signal can travel longer distance.

8. Browser is a software application that is used to locate, retrieve and display some content on the World Wide Web, including web pages. These are programs used to explore the Internet. It is an interface that helps a computer user to gain access over all the content on the Internet. We can install more than one web browsers on a single computer. The user can navigate files, folders and websites with the help of a browser.

There are two types of web browsers, which are as follows:

(i) **Text Web Browser** A web browser that displays only text-based information is known as **text web browser**.

e.g. Lynx.

(ii) **Graphical Web Browser** A web browser that supports both text and graphic information is known as **graphical web browser.**

e.g. Internet Explorer, Firefox, Netscape, Safari (for Apple), Google Chrome, Opera etc.

9. A blog is a website or a web page, in which an individual records opinion links to other sites on regular basis. A blog content is written frequently and added in a chronological order. It is written online and visible to everyone.

A typical blog combines text, images and links to other blogs, web pages and other media related to its topic. In education, blogs can be used as instructional resources. These blogs are referred to as **edublogs**. The entries of blog are also known as **posts**. A person who writes a blog or a weblog is known as **blogger**.

The steps to create a Blog account in WordPress are as follows:

Step 1　　Open a **web browser** e.g. Mozilla Firefox, Google Chrome etc., for creating a blog account.

Step 2　　Type the URL www.wordpress.com in the address bar and press **Enter** key.

Step 3　　Now, click on **Sign Up** button.

Step 4   This page shows different fields such as E–mail Address, Username, Password etc.

Step 5   Click on **Create Blog** button.

Step 6   Now, you will get an activation link on your E–mail account. Open your E–mail and check to WordPress E-mail.

Step 7   Open that e–mail and click on Confirm Now link, your blog will be activated.

Step 8   After activating the blog, **WordPress Blog Account** will appear on your screen.

10. Broadband includes several high speed transmission technologies, which are as follows:

   (i) **Digital Subscriber Line** (DSL) It is a popular broadband connection which provides Internet access by transmitting digital data over the wires of a local telephone network. It uses the existing copper telephone lines for Internet access.

   A special modem is necessary in order to be able to use a DSL service over a standard phone line.

   Faster forms of DSL, typically available to businesses are as follows:

   High data rate Digital Subscriber Line (HDSL)

   Very High data rate Digital Subscriber Line (VHDSL or VDSL)

   Asymmetrical Digital Subscriber Line (ADSL)

   Symmetrical Digital Subscriber Line (SDSL)

   (ii) **Cable Modem** This service enables cable operators to provide broadband using the same co-axial cables, that deliver pictures and sound to your TV set. A cable modem can be added to or integrated with a set-top box that provides your TV set for Internet access. They provide transmission speed of 1.5 Mbps or more.

   (iii) **Broadband over Power Line** (BPL) It is the delivery of broadband over the existing low and medium voltage electric power distribution network. Its speed is generally comparable to DSL and cable modem speeds. BPL can be provided to homes using existing electrical connections and outlets. It is also known as **power-band**.

LATEST CBSE SAMPLE PAPER

&

ONE DAY BEFORE EXAM

LATEST
CBSE SAMPLE PAPER

Information Technology

Time : **2 hrs**   Max. Marks : **50**

Instructions

1. Please read the instructions carefully
2. This Question Paper consists of 21 questions in two sections: Section A & Section B.
3. Section A has Objective type questions whereas Section B contains Subjective type questions.
4. Out of the given (5 + 16 =) 21 questions, a candidate has to answer (5 + 10 =) 15 questions in the allotted (maximum) time of 2 hours.
5. All questions of a particular section must be attempted in the correct order.
6. Section A : Objective Type Questions (24 Marks)
   (i) This section has 05 questions.
   (ii) Marks allotted are mentioned against each question/part.
   (iii) There is no negative marking.
   (iv) Do as per the instructions given.
7. Section B: Subjective Type Questions (26 Marks)
   (i) This section has 16 questions.
   (ii) A candidate has to do 10 questions.
   (iii) Do as per the instructions given.
   (iv) Marks allotted are mentioned against each question/part.

Section-A

(Objective Type Questions)

1. Answer any 4 out of the given 6 questions on Employability Skills   [1 × 4 = 4 Marks]

   (i) ______________ operating system enables multiple users to work on the same computer at different times or simultaneously   [1]

     (a) A multi-programming   (b) Multi-processors

     (c) Multi-user   (d) Multi-tasking

   (ii) __________ is a series of postures and breathing exercises practiced to achieve control of body and mind.   [1]

     (a) Meditation   (b) Nature Walk

     (c) Yoga   (d) Physical Exercise

(iii) From the following statements, which one is not correct about the qualities of an entrepreneur ? [1]

(a) Successful entrepreneurs adapt the habit of hard work from a very early stage.

(b) Entrepreneur should not think optimistically about the future of the business.

(c) Confident entrepreneur must not deviate from his/her decisions too early in case success is delayed.

(d) Entrepreneurs like to function at their own will and rules.

(iv) To remove the files of temporary folder, we type ____________ in Run dialog box after pressing "Windows button + R" on the keyboard. [1]

(a) #temp#   (b) %temp%

(c) e $temp%   (d) &temp&

(v) __________ is not the quality of self-confident people. [1]

(a) Dependent   (b) Hard Working

(c) Positive Attitude   (d) Commitment

(vi) From the following statements, which one is not the positive impact of Entrepreneurship on society? [1]

(a) Stimulates Innovation and Efficiency

(b) Creates Jobs and Employment Opportunities

(c) Solves the problems of the society

(d) Discourages welfare of the society

2. Answer any 5 out of the given 6 questions   [1 × 5 = 5 Marks]

(i) __________ key is used to reduce repetitive strain. [1]

(a) Sticky   (b) Serial   (c) Mouse   (d) Toggle

(ii) ________ means that the query uses criteria you provide to hide some data and display only required data. [1]

(a) Filtering   (b) Sorting   (c) Report   (d) Forms

(iii) Which of the following application is not appropriate to store data about ABC Bank customers? [1]

(a) Open Office Base   (b) MS Access

(c) Open Office Writer   (d) MS Excel

(iv) When you open a new spreadsheet, by default, it has a sheet named ________ which is managed using tabs at the bottom of the spreadsheet. [1]

(a) Sheet1   (b) Untitled1

(c) Worksheet1   (d) New Sheet

(v) In a word processor, ____________ option is selected for a scaled resizing of an image. [1]

(a) Original Size   (b) Keep ratio   (c) Image Size   (d) Relative

(vi) Multiple copies of the same file leads to ________. [1]

(a) Data Inconsistency   (b) Data Consistency

(c) Data Redundancy   (d) Foreign Key

3. Answer any 5 out of the given 6 questions   [1 × 5 = 5 Marks]

(i) It is a reference point for the graphics which is created while positioning any image. This point could be the page, or frame where the object is either a paragraph, or even a character in a word processor. [1]

(a) Wrap Text   (b) Alignment

(c) Anchoring   (d) Bookmark

(ii) Identify the property which help to set the number of characters in text/ varchar type field of a table in DBMS. [1]

(a) Entry Required
(b) Default Value
(c) Size
(d) Length

(iii) ___________ is designed to help users with auditory impairments. [1]

(a) SoundSentry
(b) High Contrast
(c) Serial Key
(d) Show Sounds

(iv) State whether True or False:

"It is not possible to create a default template in a Word processor". [1]

(a) True
(b) False

(v) Reviewers and authors can add their ______ to explain their changes in the cell of Spreadsheet. [1]

(a) Comments
(b) Hyperlink
(c) Worksheet
(d) Macros

(vi) In Calc, Arguments passed to a macro from Calc are always ___________. [1]

(a) Cell Reference
(b) Value
(c) Both (a) and (b)
(d) Sheet Reference

4. Answer any 5 out of the given 6 questions [1 × 5 = 5 Marks]

(i) Identify the website that offers offline blog service for free. [1]

(a) Blogdesk
(b) Qumana
(c) WordPress
(d) Both (a) and (b)

(ii) John has written a book consisting of fifteen chapters. He wanted to make the index of the book. Suggest him the option used to create the index automatically in a Word processor. [1]

(a) Tables
(b) Mail Merge
(c) Columns
(d) Table of Content

(iii) The length of the field value of text data type is _____ characters by default in DBMS. [1]

(a) 10
(b) 25
(c) 20
(d) 50

(iv) A healthy lifestyle helps to keep and improve people's health and well-being. It does not include : [1]

(a) healthy eating habits
(b) stress management
(c) physical activities
(d) less sleep

(v) In a spreadsheet using to create a hyperlink to a web FTP or Telnet, click on the __________ icon available in Hyperlink dialog box. [1]

(a) browser
(b) hyperlink
(c) internet
(d) mail and news

(vi) A _________ refers to a cell or a range of cells on a Worksheet and can be used to find the values or data that you want formula to calculate. [1]

(a) cell reference
(b) block
(c) sheet reference
(d) autofill

5. Answer any 5 out of the given 6 questions [1 × 5 = 5 Marks]

(i) Identify the mode, where we can modify in the structure of table? [1]

(a) Datasheet view
(b) Structure view
(c) Design view
(d) All of these

(ii) BSNL stands for _____________________. [1]

(a) Bihar Sanchar Nigam Limited
(b) Bharat Samachar Nigam Limited
(c) Bharat Sanchar Nigam Limited
(d) None of these

(iii) _________ function takes data from a series of Worksheets or Workbooks and summaries it into a single Worksheet that you can update easily. [1]

(a) Data Combination   (b) Data Merging   (c) Data Consolidation   (d) Data Concatenation

(iv) _________ store data in a single table which is suitable to store less amount of data. [1]

(a) Flat File   (b) Relational

(c) Mini File   (d) Single File

(v) In a Word processor, by default, evaluates _________ levels of headings when it builds the table of contents. [1]

(a) 3   (b) 7   (c) 10   (d) 12

(vi) In _______________ networks, all computers have an equal status and each terminal has an equally competent CPU. [1]

(a) MAN   (b) WAN   (c) Client Server   (d) P2P

Section-B

(Subjective Type Questions)

- Answer any 3 out of the given 5 questions on Employability skills.   [2 × 3 = 6 Marks]
- Answer each question in 20-30 words.

6. What are the advantages of the ability to work independently?   [2]

7. Name the stress causal agents.   [2]

8. What do you mean by disk defragmentation?   [2]

9. Explain any two myths about entrepreneurship.   [2]

10. Write any four roles of entrepreneurs.   [2]

- Answer any 4 out of the given 6 questions in 20-30 words each.   [2 × 4 = 8 Marks]

11. State any two purposes of using Templates in a Word Document.   [2]

12. Mention any two operations that can be performed using macros in a spreadsheet.   [2]

13. What do you mean by hyperlinks in spreadsheets? Give the two different types of hyperlinks that can be used in spreadsheets.   [2]

14. List numeric and alphanumeric Datatypes in Open Office Base.   [2]

15. Differentiate between Filter keys and Toggle keys in Microsoft Windows.   [2]

16. In which situations online shopping could be useful? Write any two popular E-commerce websites.   [2]

- Answer any 3 out of the given 5 questions in 50-80 words each.   [4 × 3 = 12 Marks]

17. Anshita is preparing spreadsheet notes for her term exam. Help her to write short note on the following: [4]

(i) Scenarios   (ii) Goal Seek   (iii) Solver   (iv) Subtotal

18. Tanmay is a class X student. He has learnt Mail Merge option of a Word processor in his computer period. But he is confused with few terms used to merge documents.   [4]

Explain the following briefly, which will help Tanmay better understand the Mail Merge options.
(i) Merge Field
(ii) Data Source
(iii) Main Document
(iv) Mention two types of data on which Mail Merge can be applied.

19. Consider the following table: Sales

Sales   [4]

Sale_Id	Prod_Name	Price	Discount
1101	Laptop	65000	2500
1103	Pentab	29500	1000
1105	Desktop	50000	1550
1106	Printer	12000	2000

(a) How many fields and records are there in Sales table?
(b) Write SQL commands for the following:
(i) Display Sale_Id and price of all products whose discount is more than 1000.
(ii) Display the details alphabetically by product name.
(iii) Display product name and sales price after deducting the discount from the price.
Note: Sales price can be calculated as (price-discount)

20. Your friend owns a chemist shop, he needs to keep records of the medicines with their Id's, date of purchase, expiry date, price, etc. in a database program. But he does not have any knowledge about the database. Explain to him the following to get a better understanding of the DBMS concepts.   [4]
(a) What is DBMS? Explain in brief.
(b) Name any two database programs which can be used to create a table and store the data as per the requirement.
(c) Which field can be set as a primary key?
(d) Is it possible to make more than one field as a primary key in your table? (Yes/No). Justify your answer.

21. Vicky is a student of class X. He used to get the work based on internet surfing but he is not aware of the internet and its terminology. Being a friend of Vicky, help him in finding the answers of the following questions.   [4]
(a) What do you mean by Internet Service Provider?
(b) Expand the following terms:
(i) WAP   (ii) W3
(c) Mention any two advantages of Networking.
(d) What is a Blog? Name any two Online Blogs.

Answers

Section A : Objective Type Questions

1. (i) (c) Multi-user

(ii) (c) Yoga

(iii) (b) Entrepreneur should not think optimistically about the future of business.

(iv) (b) % temp %

(v) (a) Dependent

(vi) (d) Discourages welfare of the society

2. (i) (a) Sticky   (ii) (a) Filtering

(iii) (c) Open Office Writer   (iv) (a) Sheet1

(v) (b) Keep ratio   (vi) (c) Data Redundancy

3. (i) (c) Anchoring   (ii) (d) Length

(iii) (a) SoundSentry   (iv) (b) False

(v) (a) Comments   (vi) (b) Value

4. (i) (d) Both (a) and (b)   (ii) (d) Table of Content

(iii) (d) 50   (iv) (d) less sleep

(v) (c) Internet   (vi) (a) Cell Reference

5. (i) (c) Design view   (ii) (c) Bharat Sanchar Nigam Limited

(iii) (c) Data Consolidation   (iv) (a) Flat File

(v) (c) 10 (As per Libre and OpenOffice Writer)

     (a) 3 (As per MS Word)

(vi) (d) P2P

Section B : Subjective Type Questions

6. The advantages of the ability to work independently.

(i) Ensures greater learning.

(ii) Individuals feel more empowered and responsible.

(iii) It provides flexibility to choose and define working hours and working mechanisms.

(iv) Failure and success of the task assigned are accounted by individuals.

(v) Individuals become assets to organisations, groups and nations at large.

(vi) Working independently ensures creativity and satisfaction among individuals.

7. The agents that are primary causes of stress are

(i) Mental   (ii) Social   (iii) Physical   (iv) Financial

8. Disk defragmentation removes all the unnecessary and irrelevant information that slows down a computer. Disks should regularly defragmented, so that the disc space can be utilized at optimal level.

9. Two myths about entrepreneurship are

(i) **Every business idea should be unique or special** Each entrepreneur knows about the need and demands of customers, so he/she can take an existing business idea and do something different with it.

(ii) **A lot of money is required to start a business** It is not necessary that every business requires a lot of capital. There are enterprises which could be started with less capital and can later be developed with the earned amount.

10. The four roles of entrepreneurs are

(i) **Organiser of Society's Productive Resources** An entrepreneur is the one who assembles the unused natural, physical and human resources of the society and makes the economy dynamic by combining them.

(ii) **Increases Employment Opportunities** An entrepreneur creates maximum employment opportunities in the society.

(iii) **Development of New Production Techniques** An entrepreneur finds new ways to save time, labor and capital in production.

(iv) **Risk Taking Ability** An entrepreneur being the owner of an enterprise is the biggest risk taker as he facilitates the capital for his idea and is accountable for his failures.

11. The two purposes of using Templates in a Word Document are

(i) Templates save time

(ii) There is no need to think about formatting while using Templates as they are predesigned.

12. Macros can be used for the following operations:

(i) If formatting settings need to be applied repeatedly in a Spreadsheet then, macros can be used.

(ii) Macros can be used to sort data and to apply mathematical functions or formulas.

13. In Spreadsheets, Hyperlinks can be used in Calc to jump to a different location from within a Spreadsheet and can leads the other parts of the current file, to different files. Hyperlinks can be absolute and relative.

An absolute URL contains all the information necessary to locate a resource.

A relative URL locates a resource using an absolute URL as a starting point.

14. Numeric data types are: TinyInt, SmallInt, Integer, BigInt, Decimal, Real, Float, Double and Boolean.

Alphanumeric data types are: Char (fix), Varchar, Varchar-ignore case and Long Varchar (Memo).

15.

	Filter Keys	Toggle Keys
(i)	It is an accessibility function that tells the keyboard to ignore brief or repeated keystokes.	It is an accessibility function in which when the Toggle keys are turned on, the computer emits sound cues when the locking keys (Caps Lock, Num Lock) are pressed.
(ii)	This makes typing easier for users with hand tremors.	It helps people with vision impairment and cognitive disabilities.

16. Online shopping is useful when:

(i) A customer does not have sufficient time to visit stores.

(ii) The product that one is looking for is available at low cost online.

Two popular E-commerce websites are:

(i) Flipkart, an online portal to buy consumer products.

(ii) Amazon, a multinational E-commerce company that provides various consumer goods.

17. (i) **Scenarios** Scenarios are a tool to test "What-if" questions. Each scenario is named and can be edited and formatted separately. It is essentially a saved set of values for calculations. We can easily switch between these sets using the Navigator or a Drop-down list which can be shown beside the changing cells.

(ii) **Goal Seek** It is used to calculate a result based upon existing values. Using Goal Seek option under tools menu, we can discover what values will produces the result that we want.

(iii) **Solver** It is an elaborated form of Goal seek. The difference is that the solver deals with equations with multiple unknown variables. It is specifically designed to minimize or maximize the result according to a set of rules defined by us.

(iv) **Subtotal** It is a function listed under the Mathematical category when we use the Function Wizard (Insert > Function). Because of its utility, the function has a graphical interface.

SUBTOTAL, gets the total/adds the data arranged in array-that is, a group of cells with labels for columns and/or rows. For increasing the efficiency, we can choose up to three groups of arrays to which the function can be applied.

18. (i) **Merge Field** A merge field is the one where we wants to insert some information from a data source into a main document. Merge fields appear with chenrons (<< >>).

(ii) **Data Source** Data source is the file that contains the names, addresses and any other information that varies with each version of a mail-merge document.

(iii) **Main Document** It is the document which contains text and graphics. It may be formal or an official letter.

(iv) The two types of data on which mail merge can be applied are letters and labels.

19. (a) There are four fields and four records in the given Sales table.

(b) SQL commands

(i) `SELECT Sale_Id, Price FROM Sales WHERE Discount> 1000;`

(ii) `SELECT * FROM Sales ORDER BY Prod_Name;`

(iii) `SELECT Prod_Name, Price, Discount FROM Sales;`

20. (a) A database management system is a software package with computer programs that controls the creation, maintenance and use of a database. It helps organisations in conveniently develop databases for various applications.

(b) Two database programs useful for creating tables and storing required data are

(i) Microsoft Access   (ii) MySQL

(c) Id field can be set as the primary Key.

(d) Yes, we can make more than one column as a Primary Key in the table. It would be known as composite Primary Key.

21. (a) Internet Service Provider (ISP) is a company that provides Internet connections and services to organisations and individuals through dial-up or direct or wireless connection. They may also provide software packages (such as browsers), e-mail accounts and a personal website or home page.

(b) (i) WAP : Wireless Access Point

(ii) W3 : World Wide Web

(c) Two advantages of Networking are

(i) **Data Sharing** Networking allows the sharing of data easily.

(ii) **File Transfer** Networking helps users to send text files, spreadsheets, documents, audio files etc.

(d) A blog is a discussion platform/site where technical (or non-technical) users create personal web pages. They are similar to online personal diary. They can be used to express opinions, share content etc. Two online blogs are: wordpress.com, www.weebly.com.

ONE DAY
BEFORE EXAM*

Information Technology

Time : **2 hrs**   Max. Marks : **50**

Instructions

1. Please read the instructions carefully
2. This Question Paper consists of 21 questions in two sections: Section A & Section B.
3. Section A has Objective type questions whereas Section B contains Subjective type questions.
4. Out of the given (5 + 16 =) 21 questions, a candidate has to answer (5 + 10 =) 15 questions in the allotted (maximum) time of 2 hours.
5. All questions of a particular section must be attempted in the correct order.
6. Section A : Objective Type Questions (24 Marks)
   (i) This section has 05 questions.
   (ii) Marks allotted are mentioned against each question/part.
   (iii) There is no negative marking.
   (iv) Do as per the instructions given.
7. Section B: Subjective Type Questions (26 Marks)
   (i) This section has 16 questions.
   (ii) A candidate has to do 10 questions.
   (iii) Do as per the instructions given.
   (iv) Marks allotted are mentioned against each question/part.

Section-A

(Objective Type Questions)

1. Answer any 4 out of the given 6 questions based on Employability skills. [1 × 4 = 4 Marks]

(i) Smriti is a brilliant student. She studies well, has joined many extra-curricular activity groups, learns swimming etc. You can say that she has too much on her plate. What type of stress she might suffer from? [1]

(a) Survival stress   (b) Internal stress

(c) Fatigue related stress   (d) Environmental stress

Ans. (c) Fatigue related stress

(ii) Anamika never resents others because she is pretty clear about her ambitions, emotions, abilities, interests etc. She also makes conscious efforts to learn more about her own beliefs, likes and dislikes. This is called .... [1]

(a) stress   (b) self-awareness

(c) self-motivation   (d) self-regulation

Ans. (b) self awareness

(iii) Sunaina wants to replace some data in her word document. Which shortcut keys could she use? [1]

(a) Ctrl + F   (b) Ctrl + V   (c) Ctrl + Z   (d) Ctrl + H

Ans. (d) Ctrl + H

(iv) Rohan makes numerous mistakes while typing. Which feature should he enable to correct his mistakes automatically? [1]

(a) Spell check   (b) Auto-correct   (c) Review   (d) Dictionary

Ans. (b) Auto-correct

(v) Ram wants to have his own business and become an entrepreneur. His father warned him about one disadvantage of this career. What it might be? [1]

(a) Independence   (b) Ambition fulfillment

(c) Uncertainty   (d) None of these

Ans. (c) Uncertainty

(vi) Swati always selects the best option for her enterprise. She has a good budget and other resources but she is not achieving success and according to her, her staff is incompetent. This statement means that .... [1]

(a) The staff is not experienced and qualified   (b) The staff is qualified

(c) The staff is experienced   (d) All of the above

Ans. (a) The staff is not experienced and qualified.

2. Answer any 5 out of the given 6 questions.   [1 × 5 = 5 Marks]

(i) A .... is a model that you use to create other documents. [1]

(a) template   (b) document

(c) design   (d) copy paste

Ans. (a) template

(ii) In a document, ... is used to apply a style to many different areas quickly without having to go back to the Styles and Formatting window and double click every time. [1]

(a) Fill format mode   (b) Formatting window

(c) Painter mode   (d) Text wrapping

Ans. (a) Fill format mode

(iii) In a document, ... refers to the vertical or horizontal placement of a graphic in relation to the chosen anchor point. [1]

(a) arrangement   (b) anchoring

(c) alignment   (d) text wrapping

Ans. (c) alignment

(iv) Tanu explained his class that to apply an existing style, except for .... , position the insertion point in the paragraph, frame or page and then double·click on the name of the style in one of these lists. [1]

(a) Window style   (b) Character style

(c) Paragraph style   (d) Cell style

Ans. (a) Window style

(v) Symbol option is available under .... group in the Insert tab. [1]
    (a) Symbols   (b) Font
    (c) Header   (d) Footer

Ans. (a) Symbols

(vi) After selecting the text you need to click the .... in the font group to make the font size larger than the current font size. [1]
    (a) Text size   (b) Font size   (c) Font type   (d) Capital letters

Ans. (b) Font size

3. Answer any 5 out of the given 6 questions. [1 × 5 = 5 Marks]

(i) Arguments passed to a macro from Calc are always .... [1]
    (a) strings   (b) references
    (c) numbers   (d) values

Ans. (d) values

(ii) .... function takes data from a series of worksheets or workbooks and summaries it into a single worksheet that you can update easily. [1]
    (a) Summation   (b) Data Consolidation
    (c) Data Format   (d) Data Chart

Ans. (b) Data Consolidation

(iii) AutoSum option is available in [1]
    (a) Home tab   (b) View tab   (c) Insert tab   (d) Layout tab

Ans (a) Home tab

(iv) Which of the following component provides additional information in the chart? [1]
    (a) Legend   (b) Gridlines
    (c) Data label   (d) Plot area

Ans. (c) Data label

(v) Which function cannot be performed through Subtotal in a Spreadsheet? [1]
    (a) Sum   (b) Product
    (c) Average   (d) Percentage

Ans. (d) Percentage

(vi) For enter the current time in Calc, you need to press [1]
    (a) Ctrl + Alt +;   (b) Shift + Alt +;
    (c) Ctrl + Shift + ;   (d) None of these

Ans. (c) Ctrl + Shift + ;

4. Answer any 5 out of the given 6 questions. [1 × 5 = 5 Marks]

(i) The .... has evolved since the 1960s to ease increasing difficulties in designing, building and maintaining complex information systems. [1]
    (a) Knowledge concept   (b) Formula concept
    (c) Database concept   (d) Forms concept

Ans. (c) Database concept

(ii) Out of the following, which one is the most appropriate data field in context of employee table, if only one of these is required? [1]
    (a) Age in years   (b) Date of birth
    (c) Age in days   (d) Age in months

Ans. (b) Date of birth

(iii) Malini wants to store a huge amount of information about her zone in a database. Her friend Gargi explained to her about various benefits of storing data in RDBMS. It helps in preventing/controlling duplication of data. Which of the following terms is used to refer to duplication data? [1]

(a) Data sharing   (b) Data privacy

(c) Data redundancy   (d) Data integrity

Ans. (c) Data redundancy

(iv) For what, Memo data type is used? [1]

(a) To add table   (b) To store objects created in other programs

(c) For long text entries   (d) For short text entries

Ans. (c) For long text entries

(v) Key field is a unique identifier for each record. It is defined in the form of [1]

(a) rows   (b) columns   (c) tree   (d) query

Ans. (b) Columns

(vi) .... command is used to retrieve data from a database. [1]

(a) SELECT   (b) COPY   (c) OPEN   (d) RETRIEVE

Ans. (a) SELECT

5. Answer any 5 out of the given 6 questions. [1 × 5 = 5 Marks]

(i) The first network was [1]

(a) ARPANET   (b) Internet

(c) NSFnet   (d) NET

Ans. (a) The Advanced Research Projects Agency NETwork (ARPANET)

(ii) Which of these services will not be provided by a typical Internet Service Provider (ISP)? [1]

(a) An E-mail address   (b) Modem

(c) A connection to the Internet   (d) Technical help

Ans. (a) An E-mail address

(iii) .... is an example of text-based browser which provides access to the Internet in the text-only mode. [1]

(a) Mozilla Firefox   (b) Lynx   (c) Internet Explorer   (d) All of these

Ans. (b) Lynx

(iv) Nick connects to the Internet at home using a laptop computer with a wireless connection. Nick is going to change to a desktop computer using a 1 Gbps ethernet cable connection. [1] Which of these should be the result of making the changes?

(a) Increased portability and decreased speed

(b) Decreased portability and increased speed

(c) Increased portability and increased speed

(d) Decreased portability and decreased speed

Ans. (b) Decreased portability and increased speed

(v) Which of the following websites is used for booking train tickets? [1]

(a) Nykaa   (b) IRCTC   (c) RedBus   (d) Myntra

Ans. (b) IRCTC (Indian Railway Catering and Tourism Corporation)

(vi) Qumana is an offline blog editor which is used for .... operating system(s). [1]

(a) Windows   (b) Mac

(c) Both (a) and (b)   (d) None of these

Ans. (c) Both (a) and (b)

Section-B

(Subjective Type Questions)

- Answer any 3 out of the given 5 questions on Employability skills. [2 × 3 = 6 Marks]
- Answer each question in 20-30 words.

6. Tanmay recently scored first rank in his class. His marks were very good but still he was stressed. How can good and bad experiences cause stress? [2]

Ans. Stress can be caused by both good and bad experiences like when people feel stressed by something going on around them, their bodies react by releasing chemicals into the blood. These chemicals give more energy and strength, which can be a good thing if their stress is caused by physical danger but it can also be a bad thing, if the stress is in response to something emotional and there is no outlet for this extra energy and strength. The good stress is called eustress, whereas the bad stress is termed as distress.

7. It is important to be in charge of your own self and not be charge of your own self and not be dependent on anyone else in life. List any two reasons for which self-regulation is a must? [2]

Ans. Self-regulation is important in life due to following reasons:
  (i) Self-regulation allows you to keep a tab on your own emotions.
  (ii) Self-regulation enables to develop the idea about 'what is appropriate behaviour' and 'what is inappropriate behaviour' in a given social condition.

8. Write about the significance of text editing in word processor. [2]

Ans. Text editing plays a significant role in word processor as it has the ability to change the text by adding, deleting, rearranging letters, sentences and paragraphs. Text editing is the main feature that users perform in word processor which typically also handle graphics and multimedia files.

9. Charul wishes to be an entrepreneur. List any two qualities she should possess to be a successful entrepreneur. [2]

Ans. The characteristics of successful entrepreneurs are as follows
  (i) **Leadership** An entrepreneur must posses the characteristics of leadership and must lead a team for achievement of goals. The leader is able to clearly articulate their ideas and has a clear vision.
  (ii) **Innovativeness** With the changing needs and requirements of customers production should meet requirements with the help in innovative ideas. An entrepreneur does not have to restrict itself to just one innovation rather he must use combination of innovation.

10. Write about any two myths and their truth regarding entrepreneurship. [2]

Ans. The common set of myths of entrepreneurship are explained below :
  - **Talent is More Important than Industry** This is not true as the nature of industry an entrepreneur chooses greatly effects the success and growth of business.
  - **Most Start up's are Successful** Mostly in the developing countries start-up's fail as they could not manage to earn high profits.

- Answer any 4 out the given 6 questions in 20-30 words each. [2 × 4 = 8 Marks]

11. Differentiate between the Save and Save As options. [2]

Ans. 'Save' means the file gets saved under its current name, in whatever folder it was saved before or in the default folder of that computer, whereas 'Save As' gives you the opportunity to save the file under a different name and in another folder. 'Save As' allows you to name the updated version with a new name and at the same time preserving the old version.

12. What makes a workbook different from a worksheet? [2]

Ans. Differences between workbook and worksheet are as follows:

Workbook	Worksheet
A workbook is an Excel file with one or more worksheets.	A worksheet is a single spreadsheet of data.
A workbook would be the entire binder, with everything in it.	A worksheet would be like one section in that binder.

13. What is the use of cell reference? [2]

Ans. In order to avoid writing the data again and again for calculating purpose, cell reference is used. When you write any formula, for specific function, you need to direct Excel the specific location of that data. This location is referred as, cell reference. So, everytime a new value added to the cell, the cell will calculate according to the reference cell formula.

14. Describe the significance of primary key in a database. [2]

Ans. Primary key is used to uniquely identify the record in a database. It can be a column or a set of columns in the table. Main features of primary key are as follows :

(i) It must contain a unique value for each record of table.

(ii) It does not contain null values.

15. Elucidate the following terms: [2]

(i) PAN (ii) WIMAX

Ans. (i) **PAN** It stands for Personal Area Network. It is a computer network used for communication among computer and different technological devices close to it.

(ii) **WiMAX** It stands for Worldwide Interoperability for Microwave Access. It is a wireless transmission of data using a variety of transmission modes.

16. Why is it important to secure internet? What are the used of it? [2]

Ans. Your passwords are the most common way to prove your identity when using website, e–mail accounts and your computer itself. The use of strong password is therefore essential in order to protect your security and identity.

• Answer any 3 out the given 5 questions in 50-80 words each. [4 × 3 = 12 Marks]

17. Elaborate the use of Section Break in a document. How to insert a Section Break in OpenOffice? [4]

Ans. **Section Break** It partitions both the body text of the document as well as partition page margins, headers and footers, page numbers etc.

To create a section

(i) Place the cursor at the point in your document where you want to insert the new section. Or, select the text that you want to place in the new section.

(ii) From the main menu, choose Insert → Section.

18. Elucidate the following with examples. [4]

(i) Goal seek (ii) Scenario

Ans. (i) **Goal seek** It refers to the act of determining your input value based on a previously determined output value. The method entails the use of a certain operator in a formula to that may be calculated with computer software.

eg. Set Cell This specifies the cell whose value will be changed to the desired value after the Goal seek operation is completed.

(ii) **Scenario** Scenarios are a tool to text "What-if" questions. Each scenario is given a unique name which can be changed and presented independently. Only the content of the currently active scenario is printed when print the spreadsheet. It is a set of saved values that we may use in four calculations and using the Navigator or a drop down list displayed beside the changing cells, we may simply switch between these sets.

19. Write SQL queries for the questions from (a) to (e) on the basis of table Class.   [4]

No	Name	Stipend	Subject	AvgMark	Grade
01	Vikas	1200	Medical	67	B
02	Boby	1400	Humanities	78.4	B
03	Tarun	1000	Medical	64.8	C
04	Varun	1600	Non-medical	84	A
05	Atul	1800	Non-medical	92	A

(a) Select all the non-medical stream students from the class table.

(b) List the names that have grade A sorted by stipend.

(c) Arrange the records of class name wise.

(d) List the records whose grade is B or C.

(e) Insert the new row with the following data. (06, 'Jack', 2800, 'Humanities', 98, 'A')

Ans. (a) ```mysql> SELECT * FROM Class WHERE Subject= 'Non-medical';```

(b) ```mysql> SELECT Name FROM Class WHERE Grade='A' ORDER BY Stipend;```

(c) ```mysql> SELECT * FROM Class ORDER BY Name;```

(d) ```mysql> SELECT * FROM Class WHERE Grade IS ('B', 'C');```

(e) ```mysql> INSERT INTO Class VALUES (06, 'Jack', 2800, 'Humanities', 98, 'A');```

20. Discuss the components of a database.   [4]

Ans. A database consists of several components. Each component plays an important role in the database system environment. The major components of database are as follows:

(i) **Data** It is raw numbers, characters or facts represented by value. Most of the organisations generate, store and process large amount of data. The data acts as a bridge between the hardware and the software. Data may be of different types such as User data, Metadata and Application Metadata.

(ii) **Software** It is a set of programs that lies between the stored data and the users of database. It is used to control and manage the overall computerised database. It uses different types of software such as MySQL, Oracle etc.

(iii) **Hardware** It is the physical aspect of computer, telecommunication and database, which consists of the secondary storage devices such as magnetic disks, optical discs etc., on which data is stored.

21. What is network topology? Also, discuss the different types of topologies.   [4]

Ans. The network topology refers to the arrangement or pattern of computers, which are interconnected in a network. Commonly used network topologies are as follows:

Bus Topology It is a type of network in which the computers and the peripheral devices are connected to a common single length data line.

All the computers or devices are directly connected to the data line.

The data is transmitted in small blocks, known as **packets.**

Ring or Circular Topology In this type of topology, each node is connected to two and only two neighbouring nodes. The data travels in one direction only from one node to another node around the ring. After passing through each node, the data returns to the sending node.

Star Topology In this topology, there persists a central node called **server** or **hub**, which is connected to the nodes directly.

If a node has to take information from other node, then the data is taken from that node through the central node or server.

Mesh Topology In this topology, each node is connected to more than one node, so that it provides alternative route, in case, if the host is either down or busy. It is also called a completely interconnected network. We can also call it as a extension to **P2P network.**

Tree Topology It is an extension and variation of bus topology. Its basic structure is like an inverted tree, where the root acts as a server. In tree topology, the node is interlinked in the form of tree. If one node fails, then the node following that node gets detached from the main tree topology.